Since 2020

HOT For This Month

Written and Edited By Paul Doherty

Mitsubishi Lancer
My philosophy of building this car was having a total package of race, street, and show.
4

Rotary Xecret 7 Shop Car
First time seeing the car in person was at May Day Garage Rice Bowl Event 2015 in Houston, TX.
12

Nissan 300zx
I knew I had to build one when I was old enough to drive, I had a vision.
24

1991 Acura NSX
The NSX has always been my dream car since I was a kid being a Honda fan from the start,
32

1993 Skyline r32
Its sacrilege to put body kits on them and lower them, the GTR is something you leave
58

JDM Calendar

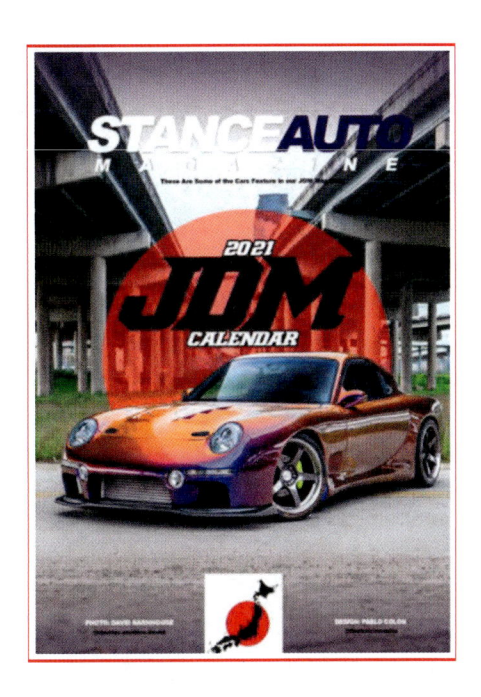

Available on:-

www.stancautomag.com

Sario Ghulam
2018 Nissan GTR

Instagram: @sarioghulam
Photographer: @fireblazinmedia

Author: Pablo Colon

Body kit: @kreamdevelopments

Growing up in Chicago my family and friends have always been into cars, buying mods and going to car shows.

My first car was a Toyota MR2 in 2010. I got really into cars when I got my v10 2006 BMW M6 and was able to modify it. I added a supercharger, full exhaust, custom tune from ESS, gauges, coil-overs, front bumper, trunk... - I love that car. I was adding a body kit to the m6 but when Nissan released its new 2018 GTR I fell in love with it and was able to purchase it in 2019. I found Kream developments on YouTube and saw how cool and unique his work is and eventually messaged him about his new body kit he put on his personal GTR and ended up buying his kit. He's such a cool guy and I have a lot of respect for his work. I'm so happy with how my car turned out like a dream came true for real.

From the AMS website :

Nissan left a lot of power potential on the table when they designed the R35 GT-R. By freeing up exhaust flow with a properly tuned downpipe and exhaust system, increasing turbo efficiency with improved intakes and a larger intercooler and boosting fuel delivery, your GT-R's potential is released. Couple that with improved cam timing characteristics and revised fuelling maps inside the ECU and the Alpha 7 elevates your VR38's output to 700HP and over 700TQ on 93 octane pump gas.

If that wasn't enough, another benefit you receive is much sharper throttle response with quicker turbo spool than stock yielding an even wider power band.

At 2500rpm the Alpha 7 is already putting out an additional 120HP and 270TQ overstock.

The kit was assembled in Arizona by @harrisonperformance. This shop has built other versions of this kit from @kreamdevelopments and was recommended by the kit designer/fabricator.

The suspension is an airlift suspension by @airliftperformance

Package Includes:-

- ALPHA front mount intercooler
- ALPHA Carbon Fiber Cold Air Intakes
- Alpha 90mm Mid-pipe (resonated version available)
- Alpha 90mm Downpipes
- HKS Legamax Exhaust System (Akrapovic or other AMS spec system also available)
- Injector Dynamics 1050cc Injectors
- Cobb AccessPORT V3
- Exclusive Benefits
- 700HP on 93 octane pump fuel
- Sharper throttle response
- Quicker turbo spooling
- Wider power band vs stock Easy to upgrade in the future

On the exterior,
I have a carbon fibre mega widebody kit from @kreamdevelopments in the UK that includes:-

- Custom front bumper
- Custom front carbon fibre lip
- Carbon fibre hood with engine window
- Carbon fibre side skirts
- Carbon fibre accent trim
- Custom rear bumper
- Carbon fibre rear diffuser
- Carbon fibre spoiler & mounting brackets

This kit is 1 of 2 so far and the first of its kind in the US.

Wheels.
Rohana 3 piece 20"

Charleston Pensa
2006 Mitsubishi Lancer Evolution IX
The Evo is known for out gunning exotics on the circuit.

Instagram: @1evo2h8
Photographer: @merrick-media

Author: Merrick Harding

My philosophy of building this car was having a total package of race, street, and show.

I realized to have the functionality of a sedan with outrageous street-able power, the Evo was the perfect fit. The Evo is known for out gunning exotics on the circuit.

I wanted a 4 door car where I can take my family to the movies, take to the track, and compete at car shows. I get all 3 with the Evo.

That's definitely my biggest reason. This car is definitely an ongoing project. Every time I get used to the power, I get the urge to make it faster.

Exterior Design

The first modification decided which set the tone for the rest of the build, was the Mitsubishi Lancer Evolution 9 APR Performance Wide Body Kit. The kit widens the Evolution body allowing fitment for wider wheels and tires.

The stock rims will be replaced with Rays Volks TE37v Mach ii 18x11 -7 offset track-spec wheels to allow clearance for the Rotora race brakes.

Exterior:
- APR Evil-R Wide Body Kit
- APR Front Bumper
- APR Side Skirts
- APR Rear Bumper
- APR Canards
- APR Front Wind Splitter
- APR Carbon Fiber Side Mirror
- APR GT-500 Spoiler
- SEIBON CF hood
- SEIBON CF trunk
- SEIBON Front Carbon Doors

Performance

The motor was built and machined by Trevtec Motorsports in Las Vegas, NV. Capable of producing over 1000WHP and red lines at 9,500RPMS with all Manley Performance race product from billet crankshaft, turbo tuff I-rods, and their HD 10:5.1 high compression pistons. Knowing this car will be driven in the desert most of its life at extreme temperatures, the car is

mounted with Mishimoto radiator and Mishimoto 2, 19-row oil coolers. A fully built ultimate ratio Shep transmission was added to allow quicker shifts and gets rid of the probability of a miss-shift. With all-round performance in mind, the suspension and brakes will be upgraded as well.

All the rotors are replaced with a lighter stronger 2 piece rotors. All the OEM Brembo callipers have been replaced with Rotora brakes with titanium pistons. As for suspension, the stock struts will be swapped with Fortune Auto 510 series coilovers to help keep the vehicle under control under heavy driving conditions.

Interior

The interior has the 6 point Custom roll cage to achieve rigidity. The entire cabin has been made by AP carbon works pillars/ door panels.

The dashboard is by Carbonetics and The stock seats have been changed to Bride Zeta-3 seats FIA approved seats to keep the driver in position better under heavy cornering.

Interior
- Takata 6-Point Harnesses
- Vertex Steering Wheel
- Works bell Quick Release Hub
- AMS Carbon Racing shift knob
- Greddy Turbo Timer
- AEM boost gauge
- AEM Air/Fuel Ratio gauge
- Autometer shift light
- Bride zeta seats red
- Custom 6 point Roll cage
- Carbonetics Carbon Dash
- CAE Ultra-Shifter

Brakes and Suspension

- Rotora Big brakes kits
- Rotora 6 piston Calipers (Front)
- Rotora 4 piston Calipers (Rear)
- Ceramic brake pads
- Rotora Braided
- Fortune Auto 510 series Coilovers
- Greddy Front Strut Bar
- Custom Rear Strut Bar
- Polished Rear Upper and Front Lower Control Arms
- ARP Extended Hub Studs
- Kicks lug nuts

Wheels and Tires

- Volk Rays TE37V Mark ii
- 18x11 -7 offset (Front)
- 18x11 -7 offset (Rear)
- Bfgoodrich Comp-2 sports
- 285/30/18 (Front)
- 285/30/18 (Rear)
- Whiteline F/Rear 25mm sway bars
- Whiteline bushings/control arms

Engine

- Trev Tec Motorsport 2.1 RACE MOTOR
- Manley billet 94mm crankshaft
- Manley Turbo Tuff long Rods
- MANLEY 10.5:1 Pistons
- ACL Race Bearings
- Balance Shaft Eliminating Kit
- Stage 5 Port and Polished Head
- Manley SS Valves
- KIGLYS Valve Springs
- Manley Titanium Retainers
- Buschur BF 280 Race Cams
- AEM Adjustable Cam Gears
- OEM Mitsubishi T-belt
- Garret 3582 Turbo
- Skunk2 Pro Intake Manifold
- Skunk2 Pro Throttle Body
- Tial 44mm Wastegate
- Tial 50mm BOV
- ETS Front mount intercooler
- ETS Intercooler Pipe
- AMS race oil pan
- Hks Radiator Cap
- Mishimoto radiator
- AUS 2600CC Injectors
- Walbro 255 Racing Fuel Pump

SHOUTOUTS

My wife & kids who are my biggest supporters. Special shout out to James Lin of Team Hybrid, Team Hybrid Family and leaders Armando/Scott and Sergio. LV Chapter Director Archie Concon (www.teamhybrid.com), Ivan, JhayR, Adrian, Mike, and David for always helping out in the garage. Amsoil, Renegade, Takata, BFGoodrich Tires and the many friends who helped me along the way, thank you. My 20+ years of Team Hybrid's Tradition-Philosophy-Innovation-Management-Quality continue making import history.

"Setting goals is the first step in turning the invisible into the visible."

Rob Krajecki
06' Mitsubishi Lancer Evolution MR
Instagram: @rgk1007
Photographer: @subie_mike

Author: Merrick Harding

My name is Rob Krajecki, from Chicago, IL and I currently work as a Regional Sales Manager / Market Development.

I currently drive a 2006 Mitsubishi Lancer Evolution MR, which is currently pulling a healthy 500whp. Growing up, my parents were the definition of petrol-heads.

From motorcycles to cars, they were into it all. So naturally, it started with Hot Wheels cars and eventually progressed into owning a bunch of different cars.

However, the Evo was always one of my dream cars on the bucket list. When the opportunity came up for this one, I had to buy it. It was a single owner car that was purchased in California and eventually traded in for a Hybrid Lexus believe it or not.

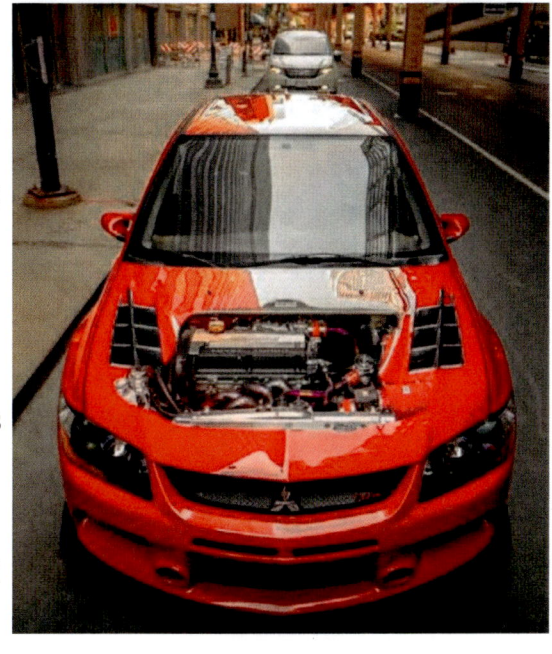

Once I got the car home, I got to work immediately. It was a diamond in the rough as far as condition goes but I was able to bring it back to life and turn it into what you see today. Many hours went into making the paint shine again since the sun had faded it to a hazy pink colour. But once that was done, the modifying began. I initially started with just wheels and suspension but it snowballed really quickly to what you see listed.

As the years went on, I decided that the car needed to be just as fast as it looked. I turned to Strictly Modified Fabrication and Eric has guided me along the way ever since. His work is some of the best in the world and continues to turn heads everywhere the car goes. The car has won numerous awards from WekFest and TunerEvolution and continues to change every single year.

Engine:

- 4G63 MIVEC 2.0 Litre;
- Wiseco 1400HD Pistons 9:1;
- Manley 88mm Crankshaft;
- Manley H-Beam Connecting Rods;
- APR L19 Head Studs;
- GSC S2 Billet Cams;
- Kiggly Beehive Valve Springs;
- NGK Spark Plugs, FP Red Turbo;
- ETS Intercooler;
- ARC (Zama Mitsubishi) Custom TI Exhaust;
- ARC Radiator;
- ARC Radiator Shroud;
- ARC Spark Plug Cover;
- ARC Oil Cap;
- Odyssey Small Battery Kit;
- Forge Power Steering Tank;
- Forge Overflow Tank;
- STM ACD Tank;
- STM Battery Hold;
- STM Radiator Brackets;
- Rexpeed Carbon Fuse Box Cover;
- RK TI Air Intake;
- RK TI Heat Shield;
- Spark Tech Coil-On-Plug Ignition;
- Tial BOV;
- Grimspeed Boost Solenoid;
- Walbro 255 Fuel Pump;
- Torque Solutions Motor Mounts;
- DC Sports Down Pipe;
- Invidia 02 Housing;
- SM Stock Frame Exhaust Manifold;
- SM TI Upper Intercooler Piping;
- SM Lower Intercooler Piping;
- SM TI Upper Radiator Pipe;
- SM Ported Intake Manifold;
- SM Throttle Body;
- SM Test Pipe;
- SM Polished Catch Can;
- SM Fuel Rail;
- Frontline Fab Cam Position Sensor Housing Covers;
- Frontline Fab Oil Dipstick;
- JMF Brake Fluid Reservoir Cap;
- Custom TI Hood Prop;
- Burnt TI/JD Customs Dress Up Bolts.

Wheels, tyres and brakes:

- SSR Professor MS3s 18x9.5 +22;
- Toyo R1R 255/35R18;
- Kics Project R26 Lug Nuts;
- Factory Brembo Brakes;
- Goodyear Stainless Steel Brake Lines;
- DBA Slotted Rotors.

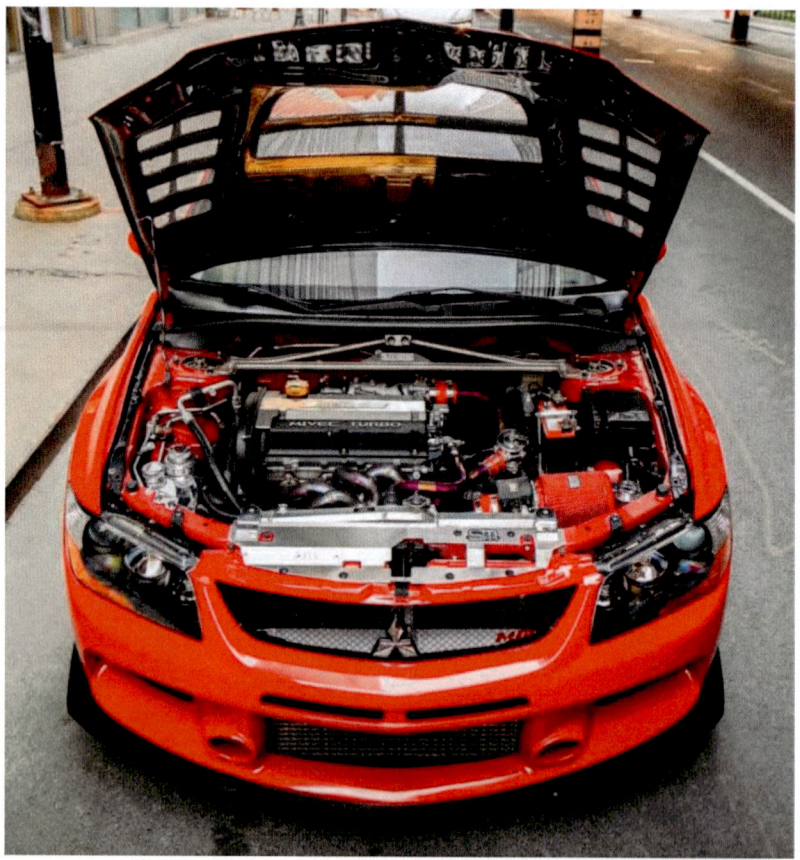

Exterior:
- Voltex Carbon GT Hood;
- Voltex Carbon Heat Shield;
- Victory Function Carbon Fenders;
- Victory Function Carbon 'Blades';
- Authentic Ferrari Marker Lights;
- Varis Carbon V2 Diffuser;
- Authentic Ganador Mirrors;
- Stubby Antenna;
- Rexpeed Carbon Side Spats;
- Rexpeed Carbon Side Skirts;
- Rexpeed Carbon Bumper Extensions;
- Seibon Carbon Front Lip;
- JDM Rear Bumper;
- JDM Evo 8 Headlights;
- JD Customs TI Hardware.

Interior:
- Nelson Carbon Steering Wheel;
- Safety Restore Red Seatbelts;
- Amerex Fire Extinguisher;
- Gruppe S Gauge Cluster;
- AEM Gauges;
- ARC TI Shift Knob;
- ARC Shift Plate;
- Factory Recaros;
- 35% Tints.

Drivetrain:
- Exedy Stage 2 Clutch.Suspension:

Suspension:
- Stance Coilovers;
- ARC Front Strut Brace;
- ARC Rear Strut Brace;
- Whiteline Front Sway Bar;
- Whiteline Rear Sway Bar;
- Whiteline Bushings.

While the build is close to where I want it to be, I don't think it will ever be done. Like any project car, I don't think I'll ever be satisfied. But I'm okay with that. This car continues to be a lifelong project that represents different phases and times in my life. And because of this, I'm hoping to continue pushing the boundaries of what defines a 'clean Evo build'.

Danielle Coppin
Mitsubishi Evolution 8 GSR

Instagram: @evo8_danielle
Photographers: @c.s_photographic

Author: Paul Doherty

My name is Danielle Coppin, 28 years old, from Goxhill, North Lincolnshire. I'm currently the General Manager of one of my dad's businesses which is a fishery and we also rent out holiday cottages on site.

I have been working for my dad for two years now but before that, I've worked with horses all my life since the age of 7. Horses are a great passion of mine but I couldn't miss out on the opportunity that my dad was offering me, so here I am!

Growing up my dad has always been into his fast cars and has had a variety of them to which include: Supra, Cortina, Sierra but his most favourite car of all time was his Ford Granada 2.8i Sport.

Although that was a long time ago, his flame still burns for high-performance cars, he currently has sat in our workshop a Mitsubishi Evolution X and a Mitsubishi GTO 3LTR Twin Turbo (Imported from Japan).

So as you can probably guess, he is the one I get it from!

Especially Mitsubishis! Being around my dad's cars and being brought up around it all he is the reason I'm such a petrol head now! And for me, the end goal was to own a Mitsubishi Evolution!

My first car was a Riced up Fiat Punto, it was the ugliest thing ever! But it never let me down bless it and was just a first car, but getting into the car scene a few years ago, ridiculous body kits etc was the in thing back then! So back then I thought it was cool, I wouldn't be seen dead in something like that no though! Ha-ha! From then on I've always had nice cars/fast cars; you have to start from the bottom right? Well, I soon worked my way up.

I've had a range of different cars growing up from Audis, BMW's, Trucks/4X4s, Abarth, but my personal all-time favourite has to be my Mitsubishi Colt CZT, I still regret selling that thing to this day.

Completely stripped out and running a stupid 200+ BHP it was an absolute little pocket rocket! I had so much fun in that car it was unreal, not to mention the memories made too, I used to take it everywhere.

To all the car meets on the weekends or to the bigger events held at Cadwell Park etc. I also had it on track which was an amazing experience. Thanks to the MLR group which set up the event MOD (Mitsubishi Owners day 2017) we even came away with a little Show and Shine trophy! (TAKE ME BACK)

After I sold the Colt, I always said the end game was to own a Mitsubishi Evolution, so I worked hard, and saved up and ended up with my 8! Which is quite amusing really as I was originally set on importing a 5 or a 6! But going more into that side of things I was getting told different things and the import company I was dealing with at the time wasn't really giving me the best customer service either so from then on I thought I would broaden my search for one and ended up stumbling across the 8 I currently have now! (Must have been fate lol!)

Focusing more on the Evo now, I actually purchased the car as it stands today! After seeing the photos of it and going to view it the next day how could I not! I was absolutely smitten with it! I love everything about it, mainly it's colour! Yellow! It definitely stands out from the crowd! I wouldn't say it's a finished project as there is always something to be done on cars isn't there! Whether it be big or small, but didn't really buy it with the intention of it being a project either, so I currently have no plans for it, as it stands I'm just enjoying the car for what it is!

Spec List:

Currently running a safe 434bhp Mapped at Area 52 Motorsport

- Kent 272 Cams
- HKS Pulleys
- 255 in-tank Walbro fuel pump
- Blitz decat exhaust system
- HKS induction kit
- Rota Grid lightweight Alloys
- Ferodo DS2500 pads
- Stop tech discs all round
- Yellow Speed Competition Coilovers with 4 - wheel alignment adjustable arms
- Exedy hyper twin-plate clutch
- Kinugawa turbo TD06 billet 25G 10.5T with anti-surge cover
- C-tech tubular manifold
- 3 port boost solenoid
- Relocated battery to the boot
- Carbon front splitter
- Carbon rear spoiler
- Seibon carbon custom painted bonnet
- MR headlights
- Evo 9 rear bumper
- Full black special edition seats
- Apexi ECU system
- Side skirt extensions

David Murphy
Boosted Toyota Celica Mk 7
Instagram: @boosted_2zz

Author: Paul Doherty

I moved to the UK eight years ago due to lack of work available in Ireland after graduating University in the aftermath of a recession.

I purposefully sought out a job in the Midlands having been to Silverstone on a few occasions for the Formula 1 in my early teens. I was fortunate to get a job in a secondary school in Oxfordshire. My current position is KS3 Assistant Principal role but still, teaching Engineering and DT.

Most of my spare time is often spent on my driveway tinkering with cars which is always a welcomed opportunity to spend time with my son. Although he is only two, he has already developed a healthy obsession for cars to the point no matter what toys he gets he will always revert to his hot wheels collection.

Having grown up in rural Ireland a car was always a means to get independence but more
importantly a way to meet friends. On weekends when we hadn't a rally to attend we were not as fortunate to have places such as a cinema or fast-food outlets to meet so most nights were spent in car parks with frequent trips to numerous forestry trails where cars were put to the test and many we unfortunate to leave.

In Ireland, there is a running joke that for any hope to get a girlfriend you had to either play football for the local side, be over 6 foot or have a nice car. I had no choice but to up my car game, I bought a BMW 318is e36 which blew a head gasket on its inaugural journey home.

Had the engine head skimmed only for it to blow months later, then engine swap followed shortly by the gearbox change. Up to that point I had only ever carried out servicing or styling mods but with crippling garage bills, I decided to start growing my tool collection and undertaking more jobs myself.

Soon I was tackling any job with moderate success but always had reliable friends to get me out of a pickle. Sold that car for a fraction of what had been spent on it, but the experience was invaluable. That is where my passion for cars grew.

When I arrived in the UK I was on the hunt for Jap car and weighed up my choices but the Celica was the only that fitted my budget of £1,500. I really liked the aesthetics of the car and have always been drawn to coupes. The car was initially only temporarily planned to be daily while I saved up for something else, hence the price paid.

Soon enough I joined the Celica-club (CCUK) and found a community to be a great bunch and very insightful. Attended my first car show at TRAX in 2014 and I was hooked to the UK stance scene.

The stance was something that was ever popular at the time in Ireland as the roads were unsuitable and car detailing involved using a broom to mop the car. Seeing the standard of cars at TRAX, I decided my stock t-sport was simply on the bottom tier of car modifying.

My initial focus was on styling so I purchased a TRD body kit and purchased a new set of rims, from there everything just spiralled out of control to the point where I think six years ago I would not have imagined the car built to have gone this far You would struggle to find any part that has been untouched on the car. Initially, the car was on lowering springs but when I figured out my wedding venue had horrid speed bumps it pushed me to consider air-ride.

The struts were custom made by K-sport in Italy and to make it more special I felt that Plush Automotive could do the install justice as their work looks incredible and I knew it would complement the car's styling.

On the exterior, I added custom extinctions to the body kit so it sat nicer as well as retrofitting a diffuser from a Supra on the rear along with a custom decat duel splayed exhaust.

At that, I had been to loads of show but always dreaded the recurring question of how much power it was running as it? At the time the styling mods were complete but the car still was running 190bhp NA.

Focus then shifted to performance gains and initially I fitted Nitrous but it simply was not enough so I decided the car deserved bigger power. I then took the car off the road for two years while I tirelessly carried the supercharger build.

The biggest drawback is that there is not a turbo/supercharger kit readily available so this entire build is using universal parts which were often frustrating as it meant numerous orders and returns until parts fitted.

On my front driveway, I uprated every supporting mod at the same time before driving almost three hours up to Doncaster with a base map restricted to 50mph.

My expectations were to be around 300+ but Wayne (Race Dyno Tuning) pulled out all the stops and returned the car with a healthy 364bhp. This shocked me as it makes the car the fastest Gen 7 Celica on stock internals.

The car sticks to the road now and with the D2 6 pot brakes, it makes a fantastic fast road car.

Future plans:

Recently I have had to think towards next summer and how I can get to car shows but still involve my son so I have removed the passenger's side bucket seat to reinstall a stripped-back stock seat, I welded an Isofix fitting meaning that he will be able to enjoy this car as much as I do.

This car already owes me a mortgage but my dream to get a magazine feature, YouTube feature and show & shine spots will mean that I am still not finished with this car. For this winter I plan to fit a carbon fibre hood and explore the possibility of getting the car wrapped in a Red Bull Drift car livery.

Full Specification: Performance

- Wizards of Nitrous 50 shot
- Nitrous Kit, pressure gauge and pipework
- Rotrex C30-94 Supercharger
- Japspeed front strut
- RT Performance Rear Strut
- Whiteline Rear 24mm ARB
- C-1 Front 24mm ARB
- D2 6 Pot Big Brake Kit
- Koho 50mm Performance Radiator
- D1 Spec Grounding Kit
- BRD Uprated Engine Mounts
- Twin splayed custom decat exhaust
- TRD Sports Thermostat
- 630cc Denso Injectors
- Stage 4 Competition Clutch and
- Lightweight Flywheel
- MR2 LSD
- Apexi Power FC ECU
- Aeromotive Stealth 340 Fuel Pump
- Mishimoto Intercooler and oil cooler
- Braided hoses pipework.
- ASH Silicone Hoses
- MWR Upgraded Fuel Rail
- AEM Fuel Pressure Regulator
- Sports M Quick Shifter
- Rotrex Bracket
- 50mm Tial BOV 3psi spring
- MWR fuel rail/ fuel return
- AEM Fuel pressure gauge
- Twin Slimline fans
- Motamec oil cooler for Rotex
- 1ZZ sump and two sensor bungs welded on.
- TRD Iridium spark plugs
- STI Denso MAF
- K&N Air Filter

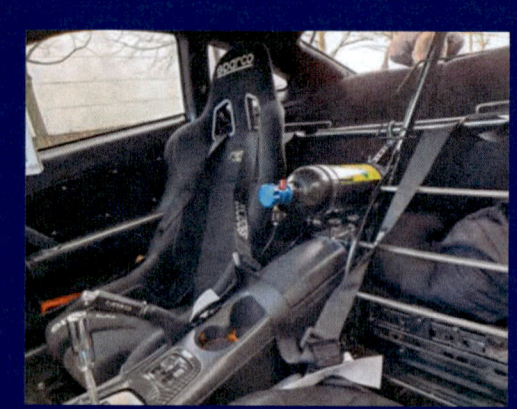

Styling Mods

- Air-Ride- K.Sport struts
- Twin chrome Viair 400C compressors
- Accuair Endo -T Air tank and E- Level Accuair management kit
- Custom boot build including hard lines carried out by Plush Automotive
- Team Dynamics 18" Pro race 1.2 White Rims
- Kumho Ecsta LE Sport KU39 225/35/18
- Carbon Fibre Sports M scoop
- Carbon dipped TRD spoiler
- C1 Front Lip
- Debadged Front Facelift Bumper
- TRD side skirts with custom lip
- Custom ABS Front Splitter with Rod supports
- TA22 Hood Vents
- JDM Side Markers
- Ingen spark plug cover
- Sports Fuel lid
- De-wiped Boot and aerial
- Carbon Dipped Plastics
- Custom carbon dipped RHS Panel around the fuse box
- TRD oil cap
- Rocker cover Hydro dipped
- Polished intake Manifold
- Custom rear diffuser
- Sports M spats
- JDM side markers
- Custom Carbon fibre battery cover
- Beatrush style under tray
- Carbon side air deflectors
- Custom headlights with angel eyes/ Halos.
- Rear lights/ fogs tinted.

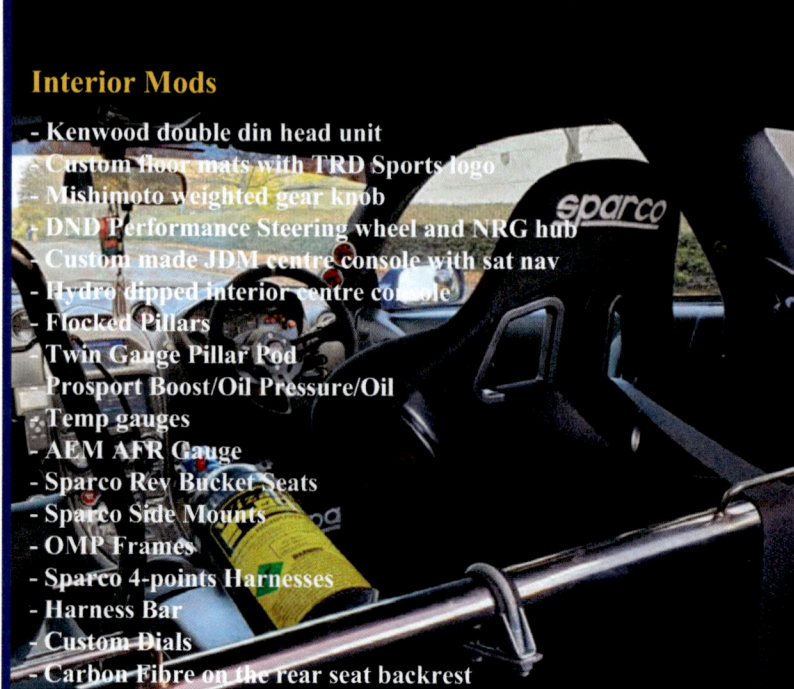

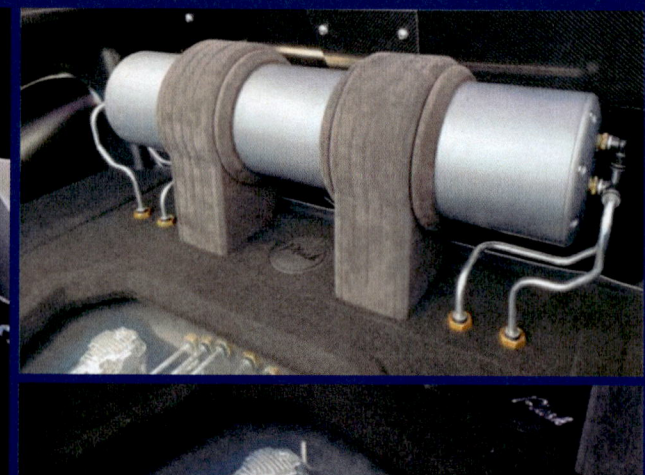

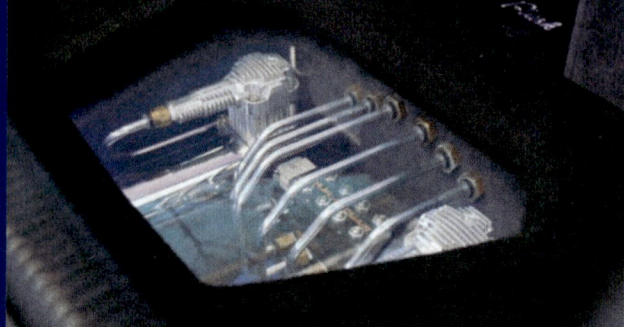

Interior Mods

- Kenwood double din head unit
- Custom floor mats with TRD Sports logo
- Mishimoto weighted gear knob
- DND Performance Steering wheel and NRG hub
- Custom made JDM centre console with sat nav
- Hydro dipped interior centre console
- Flocked Pillars
- Twin Gauge Pillar Pod
- Prosport Boost/Oil Pressure/Oil
- Temp gauges
- AEM AFR Gauge
- Sparco Rev Bucket Seats
- Sparco Side Mounts
- OMP Frames
- Sparco 4-points Harnesses
- Harness Bar
- Custom Dials
- Carbon Fibre on the rear seat backrest

Anna Brisfjord,
2005 Subaru Impreza WRX STI PSE Newage

Instagram: @BrisfjordMotorsport
Photographer: @kimjarl_fotografi

I am 38 years old and I live in Gävle, Sweden, I have a 9 year old daughter and I work as a preschool teacher, but have written a book and work a little extra as a model.

For me, cars have always been in my life. I have been playing with cars since I was a little girl. When I met my daughter's father Klas Halvarsson, it really started when we had an MDS Sound shop and built sound cars, but on the side of it were built track cars and drifting cars that we drove on tracks around in Sweden.

After we got our daughter Jolene, the sound part slowed down and we put more focus on driving. Jolene was everywhere in the garage and in all competitions and show runs.

Even after we went our separate ways, the collaboration around Jolene continued, of course, but also around the cars, Klas is one of my front mechanics.

Drifting has always been close to my heart and the sport is in the family and I will someday drive a drifting car to. For me, Cars men's family.

My first car was a Nissan 200 SX s13 that I drove on tracks, but also had as a sound car for a while. Since then I have had a few cars before I found this one.

The Subaru Impreza WRX STI PSE Newage 2005. In fact it's my dream car. I also own a Saab 95 station wagon as a daily and I still have my mother's old bubble that needs to be fixed. Sure, I can imagine owning other cars, but the Subie, she stays, I'll never replace her. I did not choose my Subaru, she chose me.

It's a Subaru Impreza WRX STI PSE Newage 2005 that I acquired in 2015 if I remember correctly, a dream car, she is a keeper.

She was not rebuilt so much in the beginning but mostly went on the track, where I enjoyed myself and developed really well as a driver about some years later,

I thought it was over with my and the car's relationship when she was in a garage fire, but we managed to get her back and then it seemed more natural that I started building on her more and more.

Got a bunch of wonderful sponsors such as Meguiars, Däckakuten - Gävle, PEAN - Sweden, Skogenracing, Werstteknik and a collaboration with the Cancer Foundation. So then I started rebuilding her.

The engine is optimized by Mikael Skogsberg from Skogenracing with 400hp on the crank and drinks 98 octane, but new plans have already been put in place.

Exterior she has had a nice subaru blue lacquer for several years so thought it was time for a turn. Now she has a nice wrap with a cosmos theme that really shines in certain lights, and because it is different and that it attracts eyes, it is a picture of me on the roof.

Me and my mechanic in Skogenracing built a brace in the front instead of being like everyone else and updating the tutors. All emblems have been removed and a grill with only grids has been procured. A lip sits on the front. The rear bumper, the number plate placement is plugged in to get a cleaner look, the plate is now under the car and a small in the front, which is easy to remove when there is a Photosession.

There are wind deflectors in the wing and mud flaps on. The lanterns are toned by my very good friend Andreas Efverström. The redevelopment plans for 2021 are already on the drawing board. Both externally and internally, so a lot will happen to her now.

A lot has happened with her events in terms of when I was at GATEBIL Mantorp with Meguiars, Modified Run 2020, been to a lot of events around Sweden and received many invitations to various events in Norway, Sweden and Finland. You can read about me and my car in Green Light Magazine no. 3 and 6 2020. And in Motorsport no. 15, 2020. However, 2020 was different but a lot of events have been done, and many new partners came. So it will be interesting to see what 2021 gives.

What has been done to date on my EJ207 engine are:
- 3 "exhaust system
- Suspension strut
- Tomei turbo
- Perrin intake hose
- 1000cc injector
- Green cotton air filter
- Walbro fuel pump
- Link G4 + engine control
- Innovate Broadband lambda
- All struts and details are painted STI pink.

The road holding is updated and built for the track. It is PEAK Coilovers but they are reinforced and updated by Ronnie Vestlund at Werstteknik.
- Brakes are specified for the track by PEANSWEDEN.
- Drilled discs
- Green stuff coatings
- Steel-wrapped brake hoses.
- Brakes are painted Subaru blue with stuff from L-M-R.

The rims are 18 "XXR and are lacquered purple by Kenneth Karlsson to fit into the theme the tires are from my wonderful friend and sponsor at Däckakuten, the rear seat has been removed and a firewall has been set up to prepare for future plans.

The car's collaboration with the Cancer Foundation testifies to the text in the rear window and also the text on the firewall.

It is a fund raiser for the Cancer Foundation in memory of my mother's death. Otherwise, as she is in the pictures, she is quite original inside, BUT even there, the plans for 2021 are already in place. The sound in the car is original except that the stereo has been changed to a Pioneer dual-din navigation.

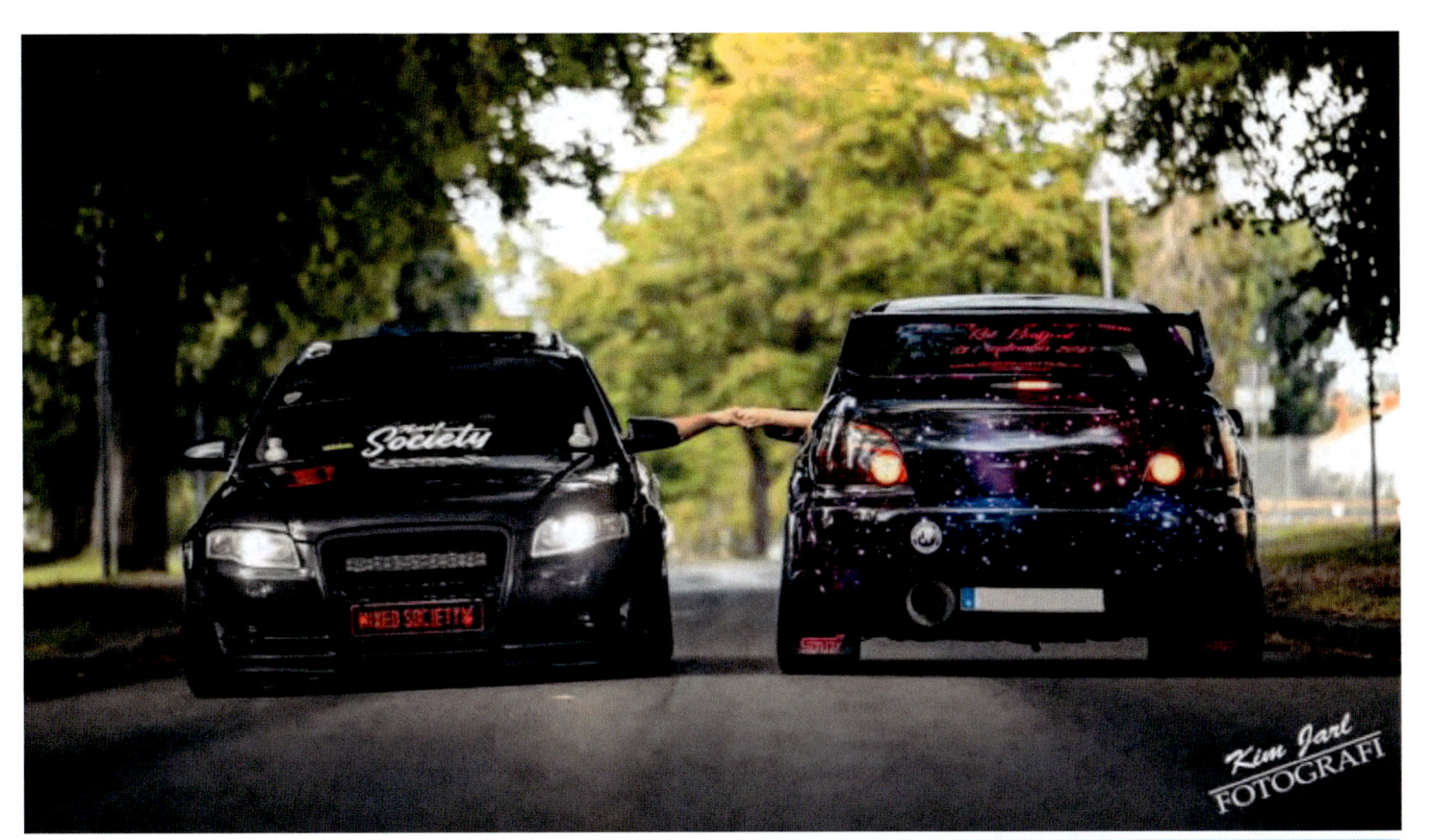

The pictures together with a dark Audi are my boyfriend's, Johannes Lundborg's car. Johannes and I have a car park with 7 cars together. We have his Audi (the one in the pictures) 2 drifting cars, a slammed mafia car, my Subaru, my mother's old bubble and the Saab which is my dailyn. Johannes is part of a local crew Mixed Society and now drives with Audin who is in the pictures. It is a slammed Audi A4 B7, year model 2007 engine is a 3.0 TDI v6 Quattro that is step 2 optimized so they are 305hp and 580nm on the wheels automatic.

It sits BC racing coilovers around and black tinted windows around. Its 12 "double bass box t3 step parquet floor in the trunk and double din.
It is an Rs grill with honeycomb and a Cupra lip in the front and 3 "straight tube from turbo
She has 19 × 9.5 ace Tyson rims

I would like to send a BIG THANKS to these People. Without them I would not be where I am today.

Andreas Efverström - Tinted headlight/tail light
Klas Halvarsson - Everything
Johannes Lundborg - Everything
Mikael Skogsberg - Engine
Kenneth Karlsson - Paint
Kim Jarl - Photographer
Oskar Gästgivar - Photographer
Ronnie Vestlund - Coilovers

Author: Carla De Freitas

Michael Skarakis

1994 Mazda Rx-7 R2 Rotary
Rotary Xecret 7 Shop Car

Instagram: @michaelllwayne
Photographer: @shutter.studios.david

Author: David Barnhouse

First time seeing the car in person was at May Day Garage Rice Bowl Event 2015 in Houston, TX. I Remembered it from the 90s early 2000s as the Famous Rotary Xecret 7 Shop Car out of Los Angeles, CA.

Few months later, I ended up getting the opportunity to purchase it from a private collector. After buying it I took the 500hp 13b out and replaced it with a brand new 600hp Street Ported 13b rew, Osgiken Trans, Diff was updated to a new Kaaz 1.5 unit as the old one had seen better days.

Total Suspension overhaul with New Custom Spec'd Ohlins were added right after. I've updated and changed things thanks to Mike at Evasive Motorsports to make it more road course friendly but without changing the History of the Ultra Rare Re Amemiya Kit.

PPG Harlequin paint still shines like it did in the late 90s. Full-Time Attack cage is in the Works and Currently at 2300lbs with me in it but Future goal is to add Dry Carbon Doors/Hatch and Finish the 4 rotor N/A setup. It's not everyone's cup of tea but I love the Uniqueness/Rarity of the Re Amemiya Kit.

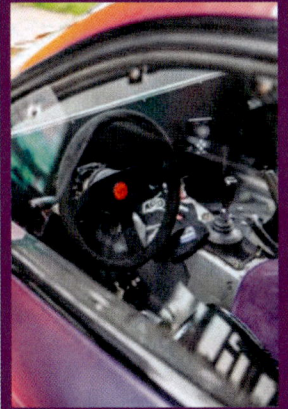

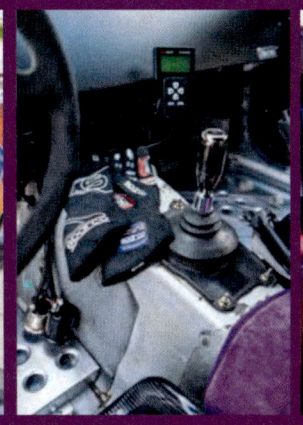

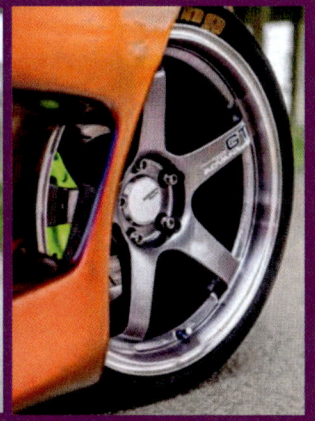

Exterior:
PPG Harlequin Paint
Re Amemiya Super Greddy
AC037 Carbon Kit
Re Amemiya AD STEP D-2 Skirts Molded
Re Amemiya Rear Overs Molded
Re Amemiya AC 987 Shaved Rear Bumper
Re Amemiya AD 9 Dry Carbon Hood,
Knightsports Mirrors
FEED Carbon Door Handles
BubbleTech Lexan Windows

Interior:
Technocraft Blue Carbon Fiber Seats w/ Ultrasuede
Titanium Seat Brackets, Takata 6 Point Harness
Momo Monte Carlo Steering Wheel
Fire Extinguisher Front And Rear
Bubbletech Aluminum Dash Kit
Bubbletech Dry Carbon Door Panels
Bubbletech Heel Pans
Bubbletech Roll Cage Mounts
Odyssey Battery
LRB Battery Tray

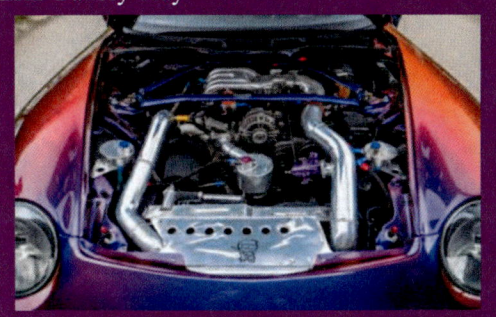

Engine:
13B Rew
Street Port
Lightened Rotors
Studded
HKS Manifold
HKS 60mm Wastegate
S366 Billet Wheel Turbo
4″ Apollo Titanium Exhaust "3lbs" Bacon
Motorsports Custom Oil Pan Xs Engineering
Front Mount Intercooler HKS BOV
FEED Aluminum Front Mount Radiator
Custom Swirl Pot w/Catch Cans Apexi Power
FC ECU
TurboSmart Boost Controller
Xs Engineering Ignition
1000cc/2000cc Injectors
Triple 340lph Fuel Pumps
Aeromotive Regular

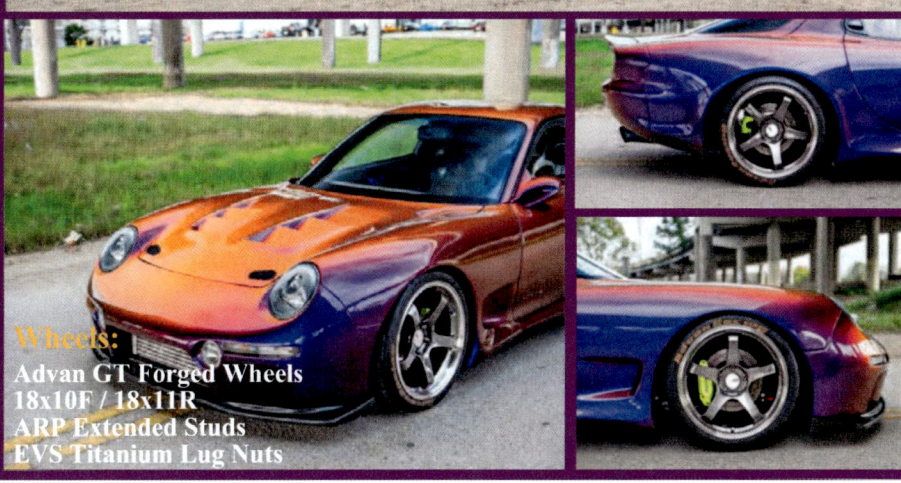

Stopping:
OEM Calipers
Endless Mx72 Brake Pads
Endless Brake Lines, Endless RF-650
StopTech Slotted Rotors
Custom Stainless Hardline ABS Delete

Suspension:
Ohlins Racing Coilovers
18kg Swift Springs F/R
SuperPro Bushings All-Around
SuperNow Tie Rod Ends
SuperNow Endlinks
SuperNow Sway Bar Brackets
Tanabe Sway Bar "Front"
Rear Sway Bar Delete
Titanium Hardware
Re Amemiya Front Strut Bar
FEED Rear Strut Bar

Drive train:
Os Giken 5 Speed Gear Set
Twin Carbon Clutch
Cs Shifter
Custom Transmission Brace
Kaaz 1.5 Differential
Drive shaft Shop Axles

Wheels:
Advan GT Forged Wheels
18x10F / 18x11R
ARP Extended Studs
EVS Titanium Lug Nuts

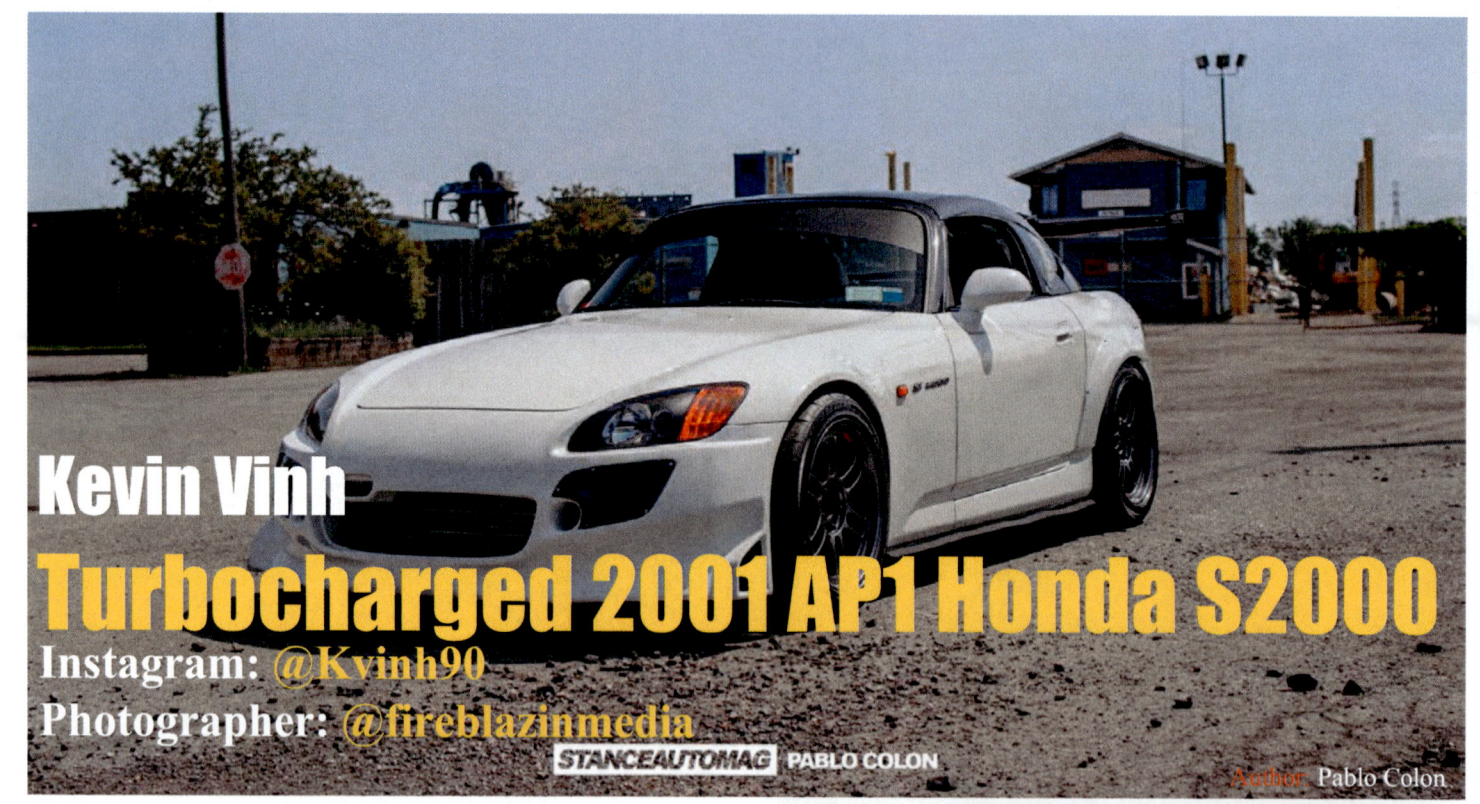

Kevin Vinh
Turbocharged 2001 AP1 Honda S2000
Instagram: @Kvinh90
Photographer: @fireblazinmedia

Author Pablo Colon

I really didn't have any interest in cars until maybe late high school, when a bunch of my friends started to drive and get into their first cars.

The S2000 always had a special appeal to me, first seeing the car in the Fast and Furious series, I knew it was a car I eventually wanted to own. A few of my friends actually owned S2000s which gave me the opportunity to drive and sit in the car over the years.

In 2016, I decided that I wanted a reliable, rear wheel drive, high revving, convertible sports car which led me to purchase my S2K. Shortly after bringing the car home, the modifications began. My initial plan was to just make the car aesthetically pleasing with maybe an intake and exhaust however, I realized that the car would be more enjoyable with a little more power.

Prior to the S2K, I owned a Mitsubishi Evo 8 with a few modifications so the S2K felt a bit underwhelming. I began researching various forced induction set ups, comparing turbochargers vs. superchargers and decided that I wanted to go with a simple log manifold turbo setup.

I started browsing the classifieds for a used turbo kit and eventually found one that fell within my budget. The car initially made 350whp/205tq on ~8 psi but of course, I wanted to Max out the setup so I discussed plans with my friend Gary Burch (who did all the work and tuning on the car) over that winter and decided that we were going to turn up the boost and run E85 the following season. The power goal for the car was 450whp however, we ran out of turbo with the car making a final number of 425whp/265tq on 18 psi. Nonetheless, I was completely satisfied with how the car ran and had zero complaints!

As far as the driving experience goes in the S2K, it never fails to put a smile on my face, providing me with good smiles per gallon! The car is very driver-focused, from the interior controls to the ergonomic shifter positioning.

I always express that the S2K feels like a slightly bigger and faster go-kart that you can drive on the street, being lightweight and nimble with a small cockpit. I've added a few bits to improve the driving experience such as coil-overs, an Alcantara steering wheel and Recaro seats.

Every little modification has definitely added to the overall feel of the car. When it comes to cosmetics, I've just simply added exterior pieces here and there that catch my eye and pieces that make the car look more aggressive and "race car" like.

I never really had a true vision on how the car should look at the end of the day, just adding to it as I go along and continuing to get inspired by other builds.

I tell myself all the time that I want to be "finished" with the car and just enjoy it but I've been unsuccessful thus far. I think that adding to the canvas, especially with the exterior, will continue up until that day, if that day ever comes, to move on and sell the car. There is just so much you can do to the S2000s, so much after market support, so many different styles/looks you can chase, it is truly never-ending!

I just wanted to say thank you to every individual who assisted me with this build and a huge shout-out to the following photographers who have taken amazing photos of my car the last few years:

Thomas Vo - @aivothom
Pablo Colon - @fireblazinmedia
Jack Li - @byjackli
Daniel Ibalio - @daniel.ibalio

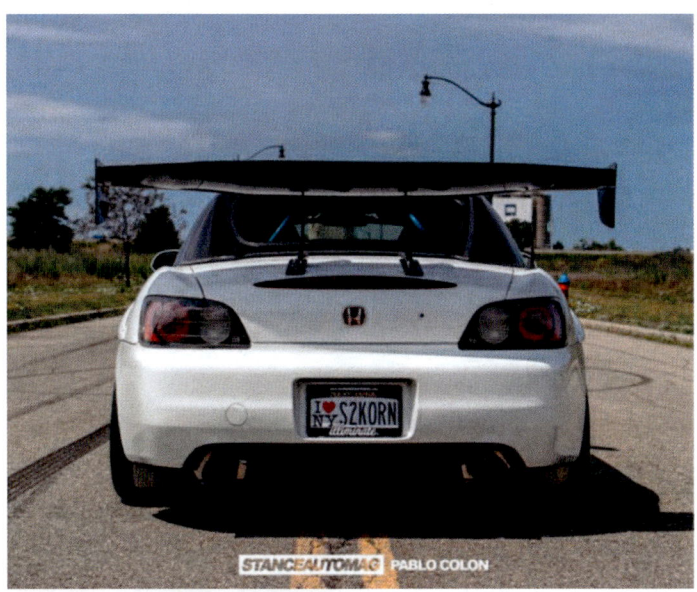

Interior:
DND 350mm Alcantara steering wheel
NRG short hub
Innovate Motorsports boost/afr gauge
Origin Fab shift knob
Cusco 4-pt roll bar
DC5 Recaros
Ap2 center console

Exterior:
Spoon style front bumper
Spoon style side skirt extensions
ASM style rear over fenders
J's Racing style rear diffuser
Mugen style CF hardtop
K1 Lab style decklid (not pictured)
1700mm Swan neck wing with Voltex stands

Suspension:
Fortune Auto 500 series coil overs
17x9+45 Enkei Rpf1s with 245/40s

Engine/Drive train:
18 psi on E85 (425whp/265tq)
Hondata Kpro
Turbonetics T3/4 .63
Precision 39mm WG
Tial 50mm BOV
DW400 FP
ID1000 injectors
Invidia Q300 dual exhaust
ACT HDSS Clutch Kit

Future Modifications:
Wider front fenders
Chassis mounted front splitter
Additional suspension bits
TE37 Sagas 17x10+47 with 255/40s
Recaro Pole Positions with proper harnesses

Giacomo Caparotta
1995 Nissan 300zx

Instagram: @snaxx_616
Photographer: @icynspicy_

Author: Joe Kohle

I'm 27 years old from Long Island New York. Growing up Me and my family were always at English town raceway.

My stepfather raced funny bikes so I was always around fasts cars. I saw my first drift car video around 12 and it changed my whole perspective on the car game. I think every car enthusiast has watched the fast and the furious franchises And I was thinking, have you seen a sick 300zx in any of their movies? No, I knew I had to build one when I was old enough to drive, I had a vision.

In high school, I owned a 95 Nissan 300zx 5 speed n/a that I loved but did not have enough money to build the car I wanted and ended up selling it over some small simple fixes it needed. Fast forward to the beginning of 2020 I began to search for a potential build. I found a clean stock body 300zx not too far from me and I went to look at it.

The car was absolutely mint I took it home shortly after. My vision was to build an aggressive looking, fast car. I went with a pmz wide body kit and with the help of pakmanz himself we created my vision. Kbd front bumper and side skirts to match the body kit and now she was wide. To match the body I got Wedz Kranze ltz 18x11.5in the front 18x 12.5 in the rear. She sat mean.

The car was two-tone for a few weeks until I had some kid talking smack saying it was ugly! The next day the car was in for a wrap. Black is hard to keep clean but sure is an aggressive colour. After the car came out of the shop I put the wheels on it and was going to stop there. Until I had a group of girls pull up next to me at a light.

They were talking about the car and eventually ended up wanting to race! She had a stock Hyundai Elantra, grandmas car! She took me to gap the city and I was upset. The next day I went and found a 1jz drop-in swap a few hours away and didn't hesitate to pick it up. I had the bay shaved by my friend Alex. We then had the bay prepped and painted candy red by 9th street auto, valve covers and grip royal steering wheel to match.

With a Mishimoto front intercooler and radiator, the car stays super cool. I put a precision 6266 ball-bearing turbo on it and she spools nicely. It has an Hks ssqv blow off valve. Custom 4 inches to 3.5 v banded exhaust with Hks chrome tips. The rear subframe was dropped and painted orange, all bushings were replaced. The differential was painted yellow. It has Brand new Megan racing rear upper control arms that are blue. Gold isr traction rods.

The car sits on green Tein flex z coilovers lowered a few inches. The rear end is very colourful. my vision was for it to look like skittles, eye candy. This whole car started as a drift build dedicated to my brother Tyler who passed away. We both loved these 300s and I know he would have wanted me to build it this way. There is more to come with this build, I mean is it ever really done?

Parts list:
- Toyota 1jz engine
- 1000cc Bosch injectors
- Lq9 gm coil pack
- Walbro 420 fuel pump
- 6266 precision turbo
- South bend SS clutch
- Wire speciality pro harness
- Aem infinit stand-alone tuned by Evans tuning
- Custom 4-inch exhaust to dual Hks tips
- Gr Kbd poly front bumper
- Grip royal wheel with NRG hub
- Nrg hub adapter
- Pmz V1 widebody kit
- Pmz side skirts
- STI front bumper lip
- Red energy 2 piece poly subframe bushings
- Red energy 2 piece poly differential bushing
- Gold isr traction rods
- Megan racing rear upper control arms
- Wedz Kranze lxz

I'd like to thank my brother Tyler Byron Gomes may he forever rest in peace, and my cousin Ben

Steve Chandler
Lexus IS200 1GFE turbo
Instagram: @Bingbloke

Photographer: @JSTE Photography

Author: Paul Doherty

I'm a Design Engineer. I'm a 41-year-old petrol head – aka: "Boomer" as my kids call me, married to my wife Nicky (who still puts up with my "spannering") and have two awesome kids Ellie 14 & Hari 12.

I have always been into designing and making things, which early on progressed into my career of Engineering and then spilled into other areas like the car scene. Soon as I could drive at 17, it was my passion to modify / change and upgrade anything I could afford to at the time.
This has led me to undertake many car projects and to my latest one.

My Dad & My mates pretty much got me into cars and the car scene, The Car scene has changed for me along the years, but always stayed a positive outlet. Growing up it was about being with a group of mates, all aspiring to do the craziest modifications or most complicated mechanical fixes/upgrades.

Everyone respected each other's builds and shared in this common passion. In later years when my kids were born, my car funds suddenly switched to the "kids funds" lol. I didn't mind as my priorities changed and I let go of the car thing for a few years, just doing bits and bobs to keep me sane.

When my Son was older (around 7 or 8) he too took interest in fast cars and things I did mechanically to repair people's cars or my own. This kicked off the Car scene again for me and now included my son this time round. He is now as much a petrol head as me I think, and both now enjoy cruising to car shows.

Even my daughter Ellie who appears "too cool" to care about cars, secretly enjoys the attention the car brings.

My Dad was a clever Engineer who sadly passed away when I was young. As a kid, I remember he could somehow fix practically anything & he also had a passion for motorbikes, cars, mechanics & anything that he could build or go-fast in. He inspired me a lot, which also led to me being a hands-on petrol head & DIY Mechanic / engineer.

So, I currently drive this Lexus IS200 1GFE turbo. My great mate Grant Journeaux has a blue is200, which we swapped the engine out from a standard 1GFE straight 6 to a 1UZ V8… then turbo charged it.. It's insane!! It wasn't long before the JDM bug got me and I had always loved the aggressive look of the is200!

Spec of the car so Far – all work carried out by myself:
Rota Kyusha 17" alloys – 9.5J ET12 all round.
BC Racing Coilovers
Wax oiled all underneath
Polybush anti roll bar
Drilled and vented discs all round
Front adjustable top camber arms
Rear adjustable toe arms
Painted callipers
Rolled arches
Metal sport trim and pedals.
LED Ring Rear lights and fogs (home made)
Ducktail spoiler painted and fitted
Bonnet catches fitted and genuine Nissan GTR bonnet vents fitted.
TRD Bumper splitters and side skirts painted and fitted
Sparco Red Bucket seats with 4-point harness (home-made runners)
Harness Bar (designed and Home Made)
Pop up sat nav converted to hold my AFR and Boost gauges (designed and Homemade)
AEM AFR Gauge and Prosport Boost Gauge
TRD speedo face (home-made)
Bride gear gaiter
Solenoid fitted to fuel flap to open with electronic push button (home made)
Race steering wheel
Full 2.5" stainless exhaust system from turbo back (Home Made)
LSD differential
Full Turbo conversion + intercooler etc (fitted / installed Myself)
Modified Sump
HKS Turbo timer
1zz fuel injectors
Fuel Pressure regulator and modified return / fuel pump
Det3 programmable piggyback ECU – Dyno Mapped to 8psi / 267BHP
Alloy Engine bay strut brace
D1 Oil catch can
Stainless braided hoses
Alloy power steering tank
Majority of engine bay bolts are replaced to stainless.
Alloy intake pipe and intercooler pipework with black silicon hoses.
Alloy ECU Lid (home made)
Rear window Vents (designed and home made).
Japspeed thick Rad
RAM Air induction kit with steel heat shield box (home made)
Starter button and ECU port installed in centre console (home made)

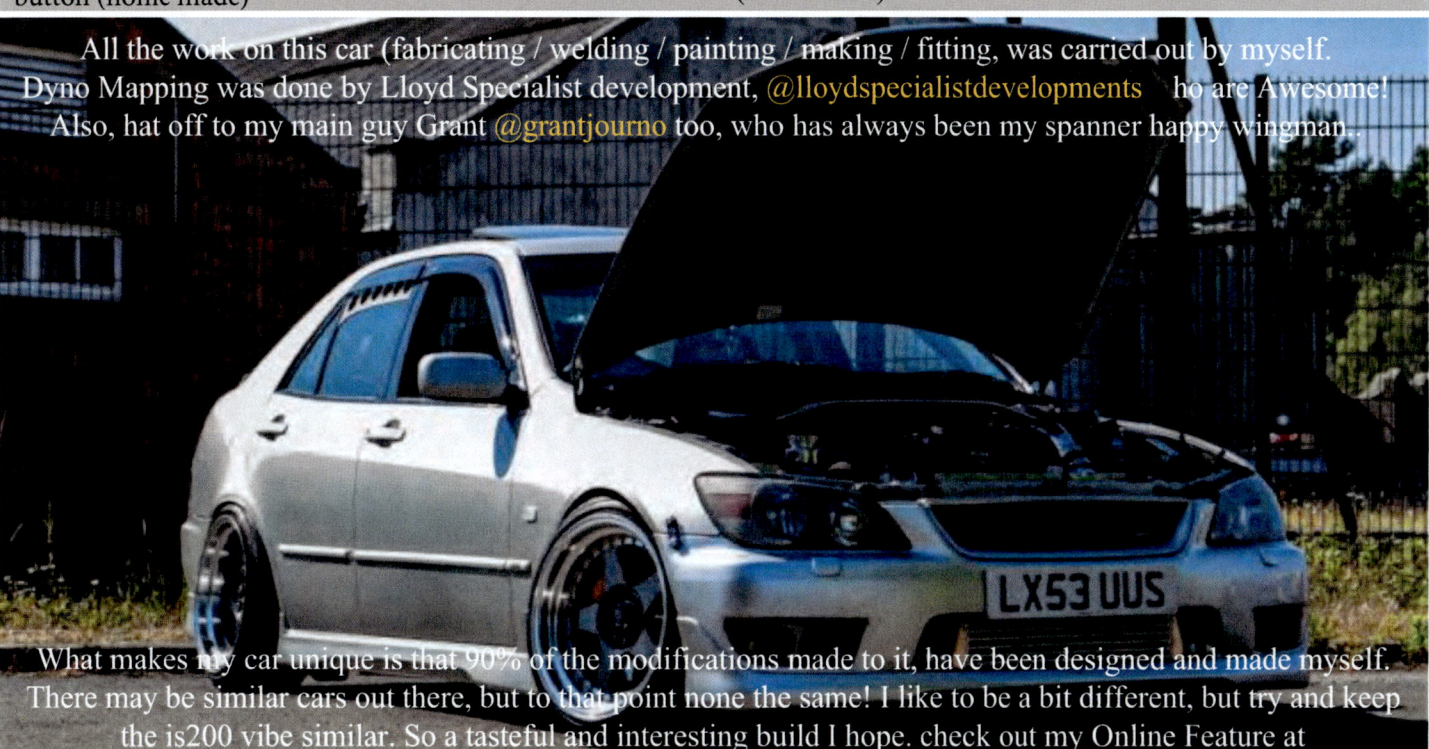

All the work on this car (fabricating / welding / painting / making / fitting, was carried out by myself. Dyno Mapping was done by Lloyd Specialist development, @lloydspecialistdevelopments ho are Awesome! Also, hat off to my main guy Grant @grantjourno too, who has always been my spanner happy wingman.

What makes my car unique is that 90% of the modifications made to it, have been designed and made myself. There may be similar cars out there, but to that point none the same! I like to be a bit different, but try and keep the is200 vibe similar. So a tasteful and interesting build I hope. check out my Online Feature at
www.stanceauto.co.uk

Jair Martinez
2012 Rocket Bunny GTR

Instagram: @Buste_r35
Photographer: @merrick_media
Sponsors: @air_lift_performance

Author: Merrick Harding

My name is Jair Martinez and I was born and raised in San Antonio Texas. My love for cars came from my dad, brothers and PlayStation.

I spent hours playing Gran Turismo and begged my dad for rides in his 3rd gen Toyota Supra. My brothers Porsche Cayman and my other brothers E30 BMW also reeled me into learning about cars.

I come from humble beginnings and I have always wanted to set myself apart from my peers. I have been involved in the car community since I was 7 years old and now inspire fellow enthusiasts to chase their dreams as I did.

Having owned a number of sports cars but never have invested so much into one car like my 2012 Rocket Bunny GTR (black edition). I am absolutely in love with the car! after acquiring the car back in November of 2019 I purchased an R32 GTR back in 2015 when they first became legal here in the USA, and after owning a true GTR, I was hooked I knew I needed an R35 GTR in my life.

I started a few businesses and I enlisted into The US Army shortly after. I knew going down this road would allow me the opportunity to finally make that dream come true. After serving my time and now becoming a veteran in 2020 I was finally able to acquire that dream.

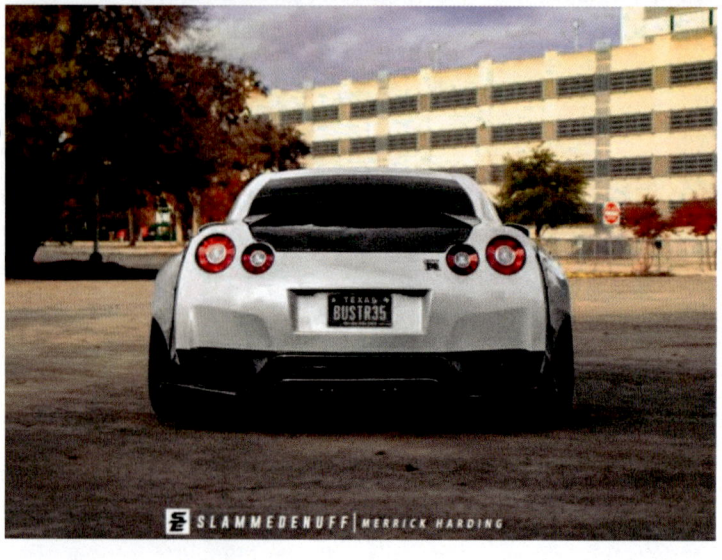

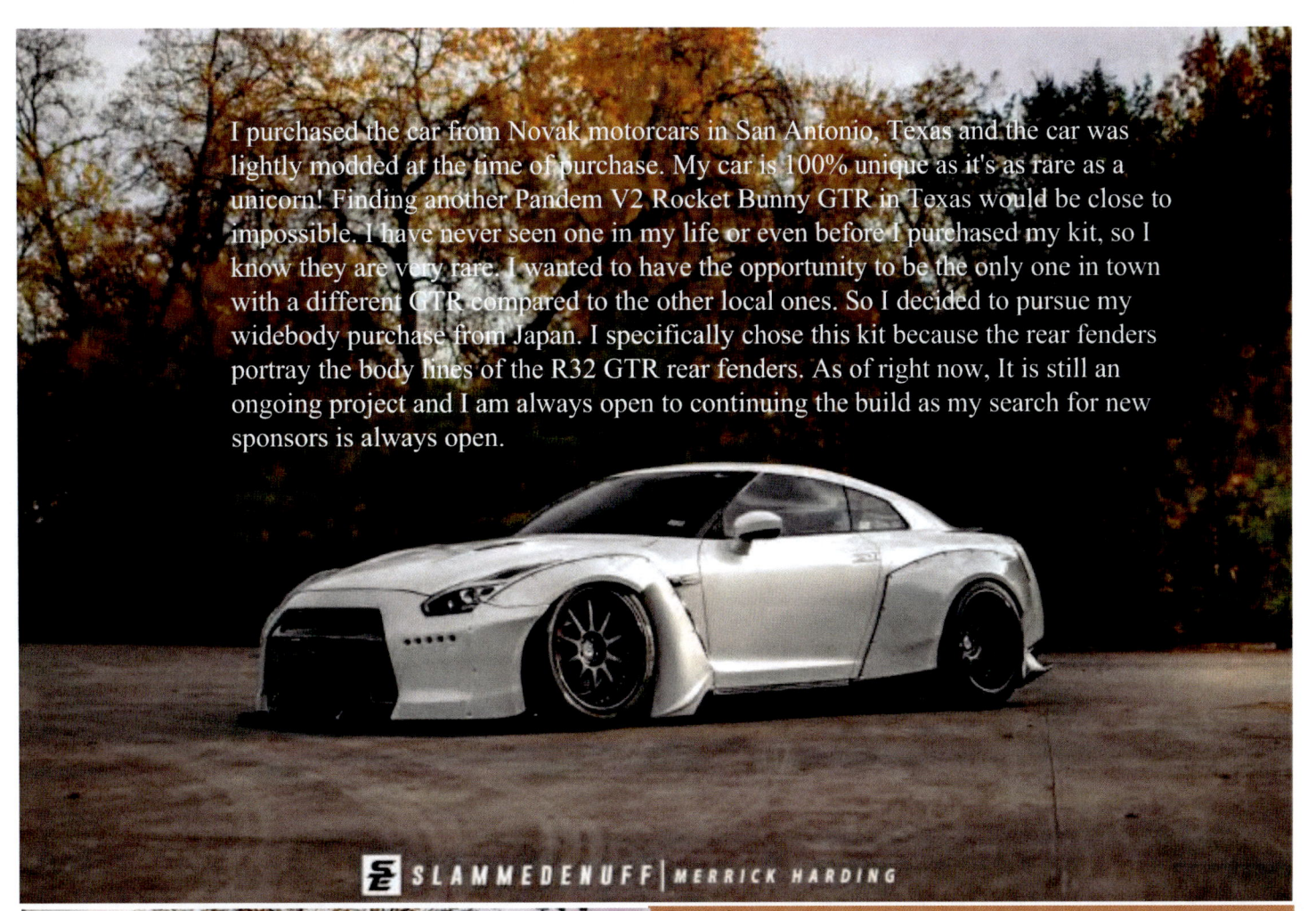

I purchased the car from Novak motorcars in San Antonio, Texas and the car was lightly modded at the time of purchase. My car is 100% unique as it's as rare as a unicorn! Finding another Pandem V2 Rocket Bunny GTR in Texas would be close to impossible. I have never seen one in my life or even before I purchased my kit, so I know they are very rare. I wanted to have the opportunity to be the only one in town with a different GTR compared to the other local ones. So I decided to pursue my widebody purchase from Japan. I specifically chose this kit because the rear fenders portray the body lines of the R32 GTR rear fenders. As of right now, It is still an ongoing project and I am always open to continuing the build as my search for new sponsors is always open.

Interior
Recaro seats. Black Edition trim.

Engine/Drive train
FBO exhaust system by HKS. 1050cc injector dynamic injectors. Go fast bits blow-off valves. Cobb intakes. AEM 340lph high flow fuel pumps. Tuned by Cobb/JMS in San Antonio Texas to 650whp. E85 conversion kit. Hawk carbon performance brake pads.

Exterior
Carbon fibre hood scoops. Blacked out 2015+ headlights. Seibon Carbon fibre duckbill trunk. Pandem/Rocket Bunny GTR widebody kit. Pandem/Rocket Bunny Carbon Fiber side skirts. Liberty Walk 3 Piece Carbon Fiber diffusers.
Suspension
Airlift Performance 3P full air bag suspension kit.

Wheels
HRE C103 3 piece forged wheels 20x11.5 / 20x13.5. Michelin mp4s 295/35/20 & 345/30/20 tyres.

Future plans
Chassis mounted wing (on its way) Updated 2015+ tail lights. Boost logic intercooler. Upgraded SBD turbos. Carbon fibre interior pieces. Carbon fibre mirror covers.

Abe Daher
1997 Toyota Supra
15th Anniversary Edition

Instagram: @sumthnsdfrnt, and @ibuildanddestroy
Tiktok: @ibuildanddestroy
Photographer: @merrick_media

Author: Merrick Harding

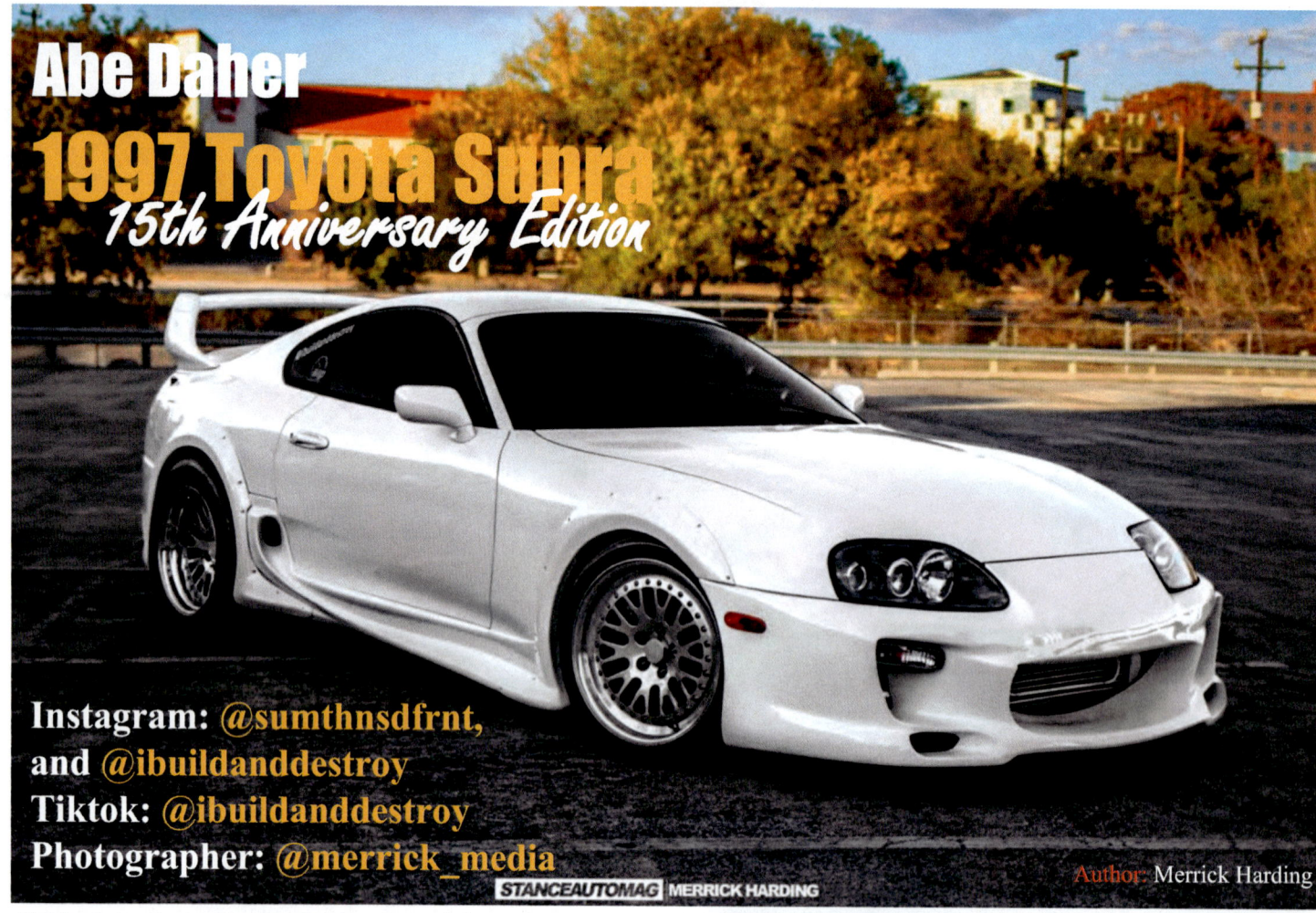

If I had to start at the beginning I would say that I was born with automotive blood.

My Dad was a Toyota mechanic for most of my childhood and has since moved on to working for Toyota Motor North America for the last 25 years.

I was 17 the first time I drove a Supra in 1996. A Customer brought one into the dealer to get an oil change. It was Forest green with a tan interior, turbo with the V160. I was working for the summer as a Lot Porter and the temptation was just too great.

After the oil change was done, I snuck out the back entrance and ripped it up and down the street a few times. The owner of the car just happened to be walking to 711 down the SAME street to get a drink. And that's a great segway into how to learn valuable life lessons when you get your FIRST job. Needless to say, that was the last time I drove a Supra till I bought my own.

This Car will ALWAYS be a work in progress, It truly is my dream car and I'm so grateful to, after so many years, be able to own this icon. The Supra is the one car I don't think I could ever get rid of, and much to my wife's dismay I still have a long way to go before it's complete.

Drive train, Built motor.
- Real street billet mains,
- ARP main studs,
- Wiseco boosting rods,
- Manley extreme duty pistons 9:1
- GSC S1 POWER CAM 272
- CROWER RUNNING GEAR
- FERIAS VALVES
- Hand made intake manifold
- Bosch 2,200cc injectors
- E85
- 3x Walbro 455 fuel pumps
- Gm Coils
- Ported real street oil pump
- Titan Motorsports cam gears
- EMU Classic standalone
- 4" exhaust 4" downpipe
- Garret GT4202 turbo
- 6" inlet
- Nitrous express 150 wetshot and intercooler sprayer
- Fluidyne radiator
- Rps triple disk carbon clutch
- v160 6 spd

Suspension
- Kw coilovers

Wheels
- CCW classic
- Toyo r888 285-30-18 front
- Toyo TQ 345-40-17 REAR

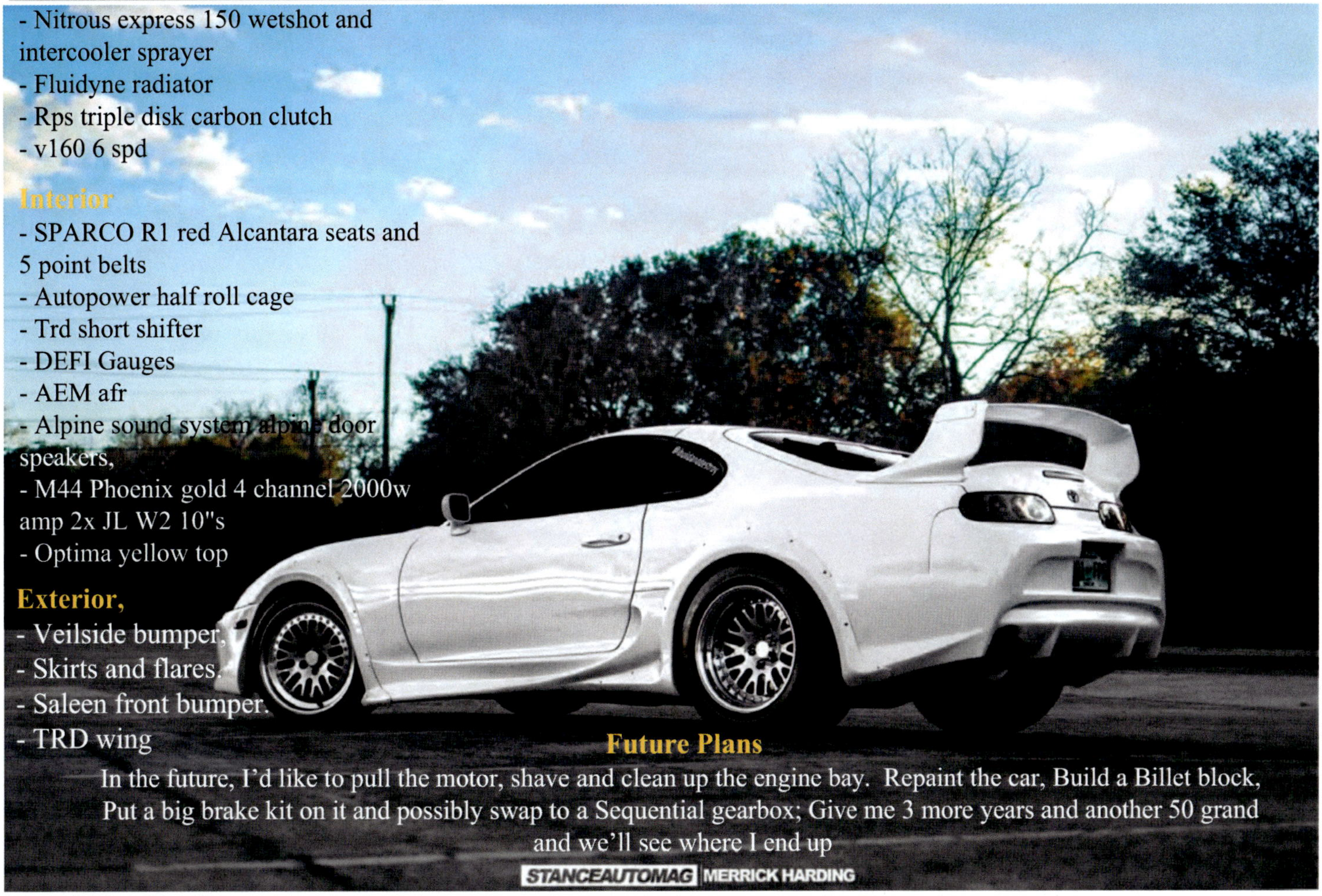

Interior
- SPARCO R1 red Alcantara seats and 5 point belts
- Autopower half roll cage
- Trd short shifter
- DEFI Gauges
- AEM afr
- Alpine sound system alpine door speakers,
- M44 Phoenix gold 4 channel 2000w amp 2x JL W2 10"s
- Optima yellow top

Exterior,
- Veilside bumper,
- Skirts and flares,
- Saleen front bumper.
- TRD wing

Future Plans

In the future, I'd like to pull the motor, shave and clean up the engine bay. Repaint the car, Build a Billet block, Put a big brake kit on it and possibly swap to a Sequential gearbox; Give me 3 more years and another 50 grand and we'll see where I end up

Jeff Nguyen
1991 Acura NSX

Instagram: @jvnsx
Team: Jade Motorsports
Photographer: @merrick_media

Author: Merrick Harding

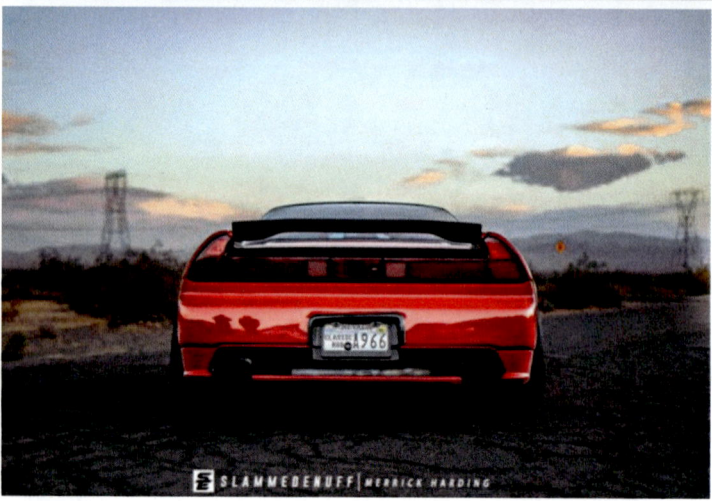

I'm 37 years old, born and raised in Las Vegas, NV. I'm an entrepreneur and currently own and operate Dis & Dat Auto Wrecking.

My car is a 1991 Acura NSX that I have been working on for over 12 years. The NSX has always been my dream car since I was a kid (being a Honda fan from the start, my first car was a 1993 Honda Prelude).

When I got the car, it was near stock with the exception of a 6-speed transmission (converted from a 5-Speed) and some after market head unit. My goal from the start was to modernize and make it more aggressive but while keeping the easily recognizable silhouette in tack.

Out went the flip-up lights and swapped over the fixed headlights from 2002-2005 NSX (interior housing painted matte black).

JDM tail lights were popped open and installed ARC Lighting LED boards. Down force supplied the front bumper, front carbon lip, carbon side skrakes, carbon side scoops, carbon rear diffuser and carbon trunk decklid spoiler. Seibon provided the carbon hood, roof cap, trunk and rear valance. Pride Carbon wide front and rear fenders make the wheel arches wider. Wings West side skirts, APR front carbon splitter round out the lower portions.

Ronne and Lou at TCM Japan supplied Do-Luck Mirrors and Spoiler. Everything around the exterior added just a little aggression and flair to each component.

Ray and Raul at Evolution auto body did an amazing job with the paint and we did something very unique with the hood and trunk... fading the red paint into the carbon. Just the extra little details that help set the car apart.

Andrew from BX Built colour corrected everything and laid down the CarPro ceramic coat to make sure the paint stays clean and healthy.

I've always been a fan of Honda high-strung naturally aspirated engines and wanted to add to it but without going with any sort of forced induction. Science of Speed's Individual Throttle Bodies system was perfect. Continuing with my theme of keeping things close to OEM as possible but adding a little extra to it.

Entire Spec List

Engine: C30A1 (3.0l DOHC VTEC)
- Horsepower: 300 to the wheels
- Torque: 210 ft/lb @ 6000 rpm
- Engine Management System: AEM Series 2 EMS
- Transmission: 6-Speed Conversion
- Clutch & Flywheel: CT Engineering Power-Grip & Lightweight Flywheel

Exhaust:
- Pride Headers
- Custom Stainless Steel Straight Pipes
- ARC Titanium Exhaust

Intake:
- Science of Speed Individual Throttle Body System
- Titanium Velocity Stacks (Mazterpiece Automotive)
- Downforce Air Intake Scoop
- PasswordJDM Carbon Fiber Intake Tube
- Injector Dynamics 725cc Fuel Injectors
- Science of Speed Crankcase Breather Tank

Coolant Tank:
- Science of Speed Expansion Tank w/ Titanium Radiator Cap (Chasing Js)

Exterior
- 2002+ Front End Conversion
- OEM 2002 Honda NSX Headlamps – Custom Painted Matte Black
- Downforce 2002 Front Bumper
- Hood: Seibon Carbon Fiber NSX-R (faded paint)
- Cowl: Downforce Carbon Fiber Windshield Wiper Cover
- Front Lip: Downforce Carbon Fiber Sport Lip
- Splitter: Custom APR Carbon Fiber
- Fenders: Pride Carbon Fiber Wide Body Front & Rear Fenders
- Mirrors: Do-Luck
- Side Skirt: Wings West
- Side Skirt Lip: Downforce Carbon Fiber Side Strakes
- Rear Valence: Seibon Carbon Fiber Rear Valance
- Diffuser: Downforce DF-R Carbon Fiber
- Rear Spoiler: Do-Luck Carbon Fiber
- Trunk: Seibon Carbon Fiber Trunk with Downforce Carbon Fiber Trunk Lip Spoiler (faded paint)
- Engine Hatch Duct: Pride Carbon Fiber Hatch Duct
- Roof: Seibon Carbon Fiber Roof with custom Carbon Fiber A and B Pillars
- Vent: Downforce Carbon Fiber Sport Side Vents
- Tail Lamp: JDM Tail Lights w/ custom Arc-Light LEDs
- Accessories: SOS Radiator Shield,
- ProCar Ceramic Coating, Tinted Headlamps, Titanium Bolts

Accessories:
- KCMachine CNC Aluminum Battery Tray
- Shorai Lithium Iron Battery – 5lbs
- Titanium Radiator Panel (Chasing Js)
- Carbon Fiber NSX-R Mesh Engine Cover
- JEGS Fuel Pressure Gauge
- NRG Carbon Fiber Torque Damper
- SOS Oil Pressure True Gauge Kit
- Valve Covers – Powder Coated Wrinkle Red
- Mugen Oil Cap & Reservoir Sock Covers
- Various Carbon Fiber Wrapped Items,
- Gold Foiled Heat Shields,
- Various Titanium Bolts & Washers & Nuts & Emblems

Suspension
- Coilovers - Tein Flex
- Front Lift Kit: UAD Variable Ride Height Cup Kit – Stealth Setup
- Front Strut: Route KS
- Rear Strut: Foundry3 Titanium Bar
- Front Chassis Bar: STMPO Bar
- Front Lower Brace: GT Spec Aluminum
- Rear Lower Brace: GT Spec Aluminum
- Rear Tunnel Brace: Cedar Ridge
- Sway Bar: Comptech 0.875" Adjustable
- Steering: SOS Steering Rack Bushing Kit

Wheels, Tires, Lug Nuts:

- Volk Racing – TE37 Saga Time Attack
- Front: 17 x 9 +21
- Rear: 18 x 10.5 +15
- Toyo Tires – Proxes Sports
- Front: 235/40r17
- Rear: 265/35r18

- Project Kics R40

Interior

- Steering Wheel: Mugen w/ Titanium Bolts
- Hub: Works Bell Short Hub with Works Bell Quick Release
- Pedals: Autovation with Dead Pedal
- Seats: Bride Vios III Carbon Fiber
- Seat Brackets: Bride Type-FO
- Harness Bar: Cedar Ridge Harness Bar
- Seat Harness: Takata Drift III – Black
- Headliner: NC Auto USA Carbon Fiber with matching A-, B- and centre bulk
- Shift Boot: NSX-R Carbon Fiber
- Shift Knob: Moddiction Anvil 2 – Titanium
- Shift Stalk: NSX-R Shorten Shaft with Cedar Ridge Short Shifter Kit
- Cluster: Titanium Cluster Trim (Chasing Js)
- Gauges: AEM Air/Fuel Ratio (Bank 1 & 2)

Brakes: Rotora

- Front: 4-Piston Calipers – Silver/ Airfoil Rotors / Red Hats – 332mm
- Rear: 4-Piston Calipers – Silver/ Airfoil Rotors / Red Hats – 328mm
- Stainless Brake Lines

- Stereo: NC Auto USA Carbon Console and Sony XAV-AX7000
- Speakers:Doors: SOS Speaker Panels with MTX 6.5" Speakers
- Sub: JL Audio W2 10" in custom CF Enclosure
- Navigation: JDM Navigation Pod with Alpine Screen
- Door Panels: Pride Carbon CF Door Panels
- Glove Box: Euro Boutique CF Glove Box
- Center Console Lid: NC Auto CF Lid with
- Mazterpiece Titanium "NSX" Emblem
- Carpet: NSX-R Red
- Mats: NSX-R Red
- Mirror: ZOOM Carbon Fiber Rear View Mirror
- SOS Double Din Bracket
- Red Stitching on Dash
- Various 3M Carbon Fiber Vinyl Wrapped
- Autovation Aluminum Hell Guard – Galaxy Black
- Autovation Aluminum Door Sills – Galaxy Black
- Various Titanium Bolts & Nuts

To top off the ITB's, Mazterpiece Automotive created custom titanium velocity stacks that are the centrepiece of the engine bay.

A PasswordJDM Integra intake tube was added to provide fresh air, Injector Dynamics Injectors feed the engine fuel, exhaust fumes tunnel through Pride Exhaust headers, custom straight pipes and out the ARC titanium muffler and AEM Series 2 ECU keeps everything in control.

Brian at Mackin Industries suggested getting a limited set of TE37 Saga Time Attack to perfectly match the colour theme of the car. Stan at Toyo TIres provided the sticky rubber. Loren from Rotora provides the stopping power with their front and rear big brake kit.

Tein Flex coilovers with air cups on the front suspension help the super low car get around speed bumps and driveways. I tried to stiffen up the already solid chassis with every bar that was made for the car: Foundry3 Titanium Rear Strut bar, Route KS front strut bar, GT Spec front and rear braces, Cedar Ridge tunnel brace, and STMPO front chassis brace.

Interior, an ongoing theme continues more carbon and titanium. Bun from @LotUSA supplied Bride Vios buckets (in the carbon of course) and Takata harnesses lock me in place. Mugen suede wheel that's linked via Works Bell hub and quick release.

Pride Carbon, NC Auto and Euroboutique give the interior more carbon treatment (carbon door panels by Pride Carbon while the Carbon headliner, centre console lid, centre radio stack, A and B pillars are by NC Auto and the Carbon glove box is by @Euroboutique).

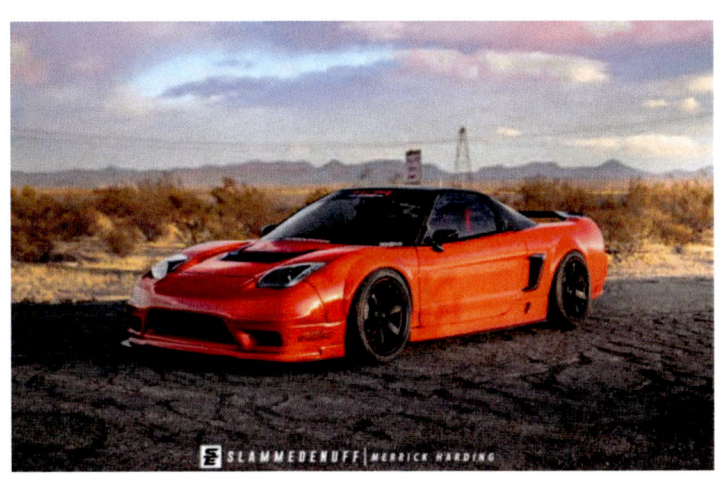

At the end of it all, a certain theme kept emerging and that's carbon and titanium details. This by far my favourite iteration of the car so far and I think I just want to enjoy it for now.

I can't thank everyone that helped me make this project come to the realization and also all the friends I've met at meets, shows, drives and throughout the build.

Sponsors/Shout Outs:
My crew at Dis & Dat Auto
My team Jade Motorsports
Henry at 3W Distributing
Ray and Raul at Evolution Auto Body Ronne and Lou at TCM Japan Brian at Mackin Industries
Stan at Toyo Tires
Bun at Lot USA/Bride
Loren at Rotora
Thomas at Downforce
Mark at Pride Group
Andrew at BX Built
Jake at Masterpiece Automotive Meguiar's
Charlie and Suzi at Vinyl Empire 702

My parents
And most of all my love:
Tahnee and my son: Jax

Ronne Medina
2006 Subaru Impreza WRX STI (GDB-F)

Instagram: @Battleborn_STi
Photographer: @merrick_media

Author: Merrick Harding

I am like most modern enthusiasts – just a regular guy with an expensive hobby. I am also a small business owner, husband, father, and veteran. While still trying to wrap my life around the previous sentence, I am also enrolled in school full time.

So, late in my life, after serving this beautiful country for 8 years, I ventured into an attempt to finish a college degree that has nothing to do with my resume, but has many to do with my personal goal. I've always wanted to acquire a degree and with the distraction of the military life, cars, and family, I put that goal to rest. So, here I am, wiser and lighter (fewer benjamins in my pocket), but happier with a full house. We reside in Las Vegas, where we now call home, but the future is bright, and it may lead us elsewhere. However, I am kind of in the perfect spot in my life right now in terms of growth, automotive, and personal spirit.

I try not to make multiple features sound so textbook, with copy and paste answers, but you know, it has always started with the Honda scene – and the scene out here in Vegas, at the time (era 2003-2007) was really big. Like, "no one cared you had a cool show car with an LS1 swap and collected trophies, bro, with your hard parked duraflex body kit" it really was like a fast and furious showdown every Thursday and Saturday nights. These nights were when car teams/clubs/groups, actually put the drama to rest, or maybe even stirred more drama.

They raced at a 1,320-foot distance, from start to finish, you brought it there and left it all at the raceway, illegally of course. This was intense stuff, and I mean, seriously intense. Each Thursday or Saturday night would be 200+ cars gathered and people raced. This was something that definitely led me into this habitual content of the automotive building.

As cliché as it is, I've always wanted to own a 4-cylinder turbo'd Japanese vehicle – that was a mouthful huh? The choices were clear at the time, coming on my latest tenure in the Navy, I decided to treat myself with something I've always wanted, but the options were very open. I was shopping for months for an Evo IX, but the more and more I kept looking, the more I hated looking .

The Evo interior is just so bland like it needs some pumpkin spice update to it, and I didn't really care for the irony of the 4G63, because I wouldn't be staring at the engine while driving, I'd be stuck with the after taste of vomit staring at the interior.

Then, one day, I had a friend text me asking if I was still interested in his STi, as it sat in the garage for years due to his craziness in back-to-back deployments.

I didn't hesitate, I knew it was well taken care of, well, just not driven enough. So that's a quick glimpse of how it all started.

The mod sheet is not as extensive as I want it to be, but I think the fun of actually owning an older Subaru versus your modern 2015+ WRX or STi, is that there is a heritage to follow with it. That's where I went with my theme for my car.

You can't find discontinued parts on a fairly new car, especially grassroots name brands such as ARC, ZERO SPORTS, or some of the old Tommy Kaira, and such products. I know zero sports is still in production for the newer models, but it's the little collectable things that you just can't replicate and say, "its rare." – that term only works if it was actually genuine, found, and resurrected.

Purely opinionated based of course, but also, I am personally not into the new Subaru's. As cool as they are, and I've personally been a part of some SEMA builds for the newer chassis, it just doesn't seem to be something you'd see in my driveway.

Aside from the previous notion, looking more at the car build is really taking some of the OG to look mixed with modern-day vibes, and splattering carbon fibre into the canvas, and the final product you end up with is a little something like my car.

What made me buy this car, it was just the right timing – From searching for a turbocharged car and my friend selling his barely used car, I think it fell in my hands at the right time.

I don't look back or regret anything either and I think what honestly makes it very unique, is the way I envisioned the widebody to come to real life.

I'll probably hurt some feelings here, but riveted or screwed on fender flares, even how some widebody kits come, just aren't appealing to me.

The way we did this widebody, and moulding the OEM 05-07 STI fender flare to it, creating the body to look very natural, but wider, is what really emphasizes the uniqueness.

The painter who did the bodywork, really killed it, nonetheless. I am thankful for how the bodywork I envisioned, actually came to real life. Is it finished or an ongoing project if any enthusiast ever says his project is finished, he/she is a damn liar?

It may be currently postponed, whether it be due to budget, lack of interest, or any matter whatsoever, but to say it's finished, I'd be lying to myself. I have plans for other things, but for now, it's on a decent break – life is hitting priorities at the moment.

Specs Sheet:-

INTERIOR & ELECTRONICS

- DEFI Tri-Gauge Center Dash Pod Mount
- CR Advance 60mm, Boost
- CR Advance 60mm, Oil Pressure
- CR Advance 60mm, Exhaust Temperature
- AEM UEGO Wide Band Air/Fuel Ratio (AFR), 52mm Digital Meter
- PIONEER AVIC-F900BT
- Viper 5901 Auto Security Systems
- Works Bell Steering Wheel Hub Adapter
- Works Bell/Night runner Collab Rapfix GTC Steering Wheel Tilt System
- Personal Neo Grinta – 325mm Steering Wheel
- Prodrive Japan – Discontinued and rare 4-point harness
- Recaro Rafael Red Wildcat SR5, 1 of 500 made
- OE Subaru JDM – Door Sills with Unhinged Labs STi Badge
- OE Subaru JDM – Red HVAC w/ Subtle Solutions Black Overlay
- OE Subaru JDM – Red Hazard Switch
- ILLUMAESTHETIC – Custom Mature Gauge Cluster
- Top Stitch Trim – "Gucci" Center Arm Rest
- Top Stitch Trim – "Gucci" Shift Boot
- Carbon Fiber WRC Door Cards
- Carbon Fiber Kevlar Rear Seat Delete
- Carbon Fiber Kevlar Rear Firewall
- Carbon Fiber Kevlar Rear Upper C Pillar Compartment
- Carbon Fiber A-Pillar covers
- Carbon Fiber Lower A-Pillar covers
- Carbon Fiber JDM C-Pillar covers
- Carbon Fiber AC Vents
- Carbon Fiber Clock/Gauge Pod
- Carbon Fiber Cluster Gauge
- Carbon Fiber Steering Wheel Trim
- Flocked Lower Dash
- Alcantara Headliner
- Trunk build, both myself and 14yr old son put it all together Sound stream Subwoofer 10" (x2) and Sound stream Amplifier setup
- Lathe - Werks Complete Interior Titanium Trim (Shift Knob, HVAC knobs, E-Brake, Boot Collar, etc.)

ENGINE MODIFICATIONS

- Odyssey PC680 Battery, with mounting bracket
- Engine: Subaru EJ257, 2.5T
- Horsepower: 376 all-wheel horsepower
- Torque: 365 all-wheel ft/lb
- Tuning – Church Automotive Testing
- Engine Management System: COBB Tuning
- Clutch: SPEC Stage 2+ equipped with SPEC Steel Flywheel
- Headers: OEM Port Matched
- Intake: Injen Performance Piping Paired with HKS Super Induction Filter
- Aeromotive Fuel Pump
- Deatshworks 1000cc Fuel Injector- Grimmspeed Phenolic Intake Manifold Spacer, 3mm
- Mishimoto Silicone Inlet Induction Silicone
- Extreme turbo system Front Mount Intercooler
- Tial sport Q50 – Blow off valve
- Perrin Performance Downpipe
- JDM Prova Oil Cap
- Perrin Engine Mounts 
- Grimmspeed Up-pipe with Grimmspeed Wastegate Bracket
- Exhaust: Tomei Expreme Ti, JDM Version (Straight exit)
- Additional Engine Modifications:
- Crawford Performance Air/Oil Separator, Closed-loop system
- Killer B Motorsports Ultimate Oil Pickup
- OE Subaru 11mm Oil Pump Upgrade (2006 STI uses standard 10mm)
- Tial sport38mm External Wastegate, with Lower Dump Tube.
- COBB Electronic Boost Controller
- KOYO Radiator with JDM Rare Zero Sports Radiator Cap, and Zero Sports Upper Hose
- JDM ARC Titanium upper radiator cap
- JDM Kakumei Radiator Cooling Panel
- JDM ARC Titanium Alternator Cover

EXTERIOR MODIFICATIONS:-
- L'aunsport WRC Wide Body with OEM 05-07 STi Fender Flares Molded
- L'aunsport Carbon Fiber Exterior B Pillar
- L'aunsport Carbon Fiber Exterior C Pillar
- Mature Japan – Front Bumper
- Mature Japan – Carbon Fiber Rear Diffuser
- Charge speed Type 2 Side Skirts, with titanium badge & carbon fibre extensions
- Charge speed Carbon Fiber Roof Vane
- MRacing Carbon Fiber Type 4 Side Mirrors (As seen on the Cusco Japan Time Attack Car)
kaminari Reverse Scoop Carbon Fiber Hood
- VOLTEX – Type 2 GT Wing, 1700mm, 295mm stands
- VIS RACING Demon Carbon Fiber Trunk
- 2004/2005 WRX Tail Lamps, JDM rewire
- OE Subaru JDM Headlights - *TSX-R Headlight Projector Upgrade
- OE Subaru JDM Side Markers
- OE Subaru JDM SPEC C Roof Vent
- Carbon Fiber Windshield Cowl

SUSPENSION & BRAKES
- Coilovers: Fortune Auto APLS
- Custom Springs Rates: Swift Springs F14k/R16k
- Air Piston Lift System equipped in front (Air Cups)
- SPC Front and Rear Camber Bolts
- ROTORA Japan Full Big Brake Kit
- OKUYAMA/CARBING Front Strut Tower with Master Cylinder Brace
- WHITELINE Performance Anti-lift Kit
- WHITELINE Performance Sway Bars & End Links
- KARTBOY Engineering – Shifter Bushings
- KARTBOY Engineering – Transmission Cross member Bushings
- GROUP-N Transmission Mount
- BEATRUSH/LAILE Pitch Stop Mount
- BEATRUSH/LAILE Rear Cabin Foot Brace
- OKUYAMA/CARBING – 11 Point Roll Bar

- Prodrive– Differential cover plate

Wheels:-
- Rays volks racing – CE28N 18x10.5 +18
- EVS Racing Titanium Lug Nuts
- TOYO Tires R888R 295/30/18

Shout Outs:-
I wish to give my sincere thanks to my Partners at TCM JAPAN, Lou B. & Allan A. for everything they've done to stick by my side during this build, and allowing me to grow better in the business world, and being such great mentors in my life. Secondly, I wish to thank my long-time friend and fellow business partner Jeffrey N. at Dis & DAT for his personal insights in the automotive world and also helping me become a better, well-rounded entrepreneur. Next, to my sponsors and some great friends in other businesses who have either allowed me to be part of their elite team, or have created a foundation of friendship that can be trusted for a prolonged tenure.

Devin & Terry at Fortune Auto USA, Eita at L'aunsport Japan
Rajeet & Takashi at Mastermind North America
Jake with HVY Composites in the UK, Alan Kohler at Odyssey Battery
Loren with Rotora Inc, KJ Takahashi, owner of My Japan Direct, Fred V. & Chris at VIS Racing,
Stan at Toyo Tires, Blackvue Dash Cam Team, CY Lee at Evasive Motorsports

Saving the best for last: To my Wife, Tiffany, and my Kids. The countless hours in the garage, turning wrenches when I could be inside and spending memories with you all, you choose to continue and support my hobby and allow me to follow what you feel makes me happy. The care that you all give and the love that I feel from you, all is more than enough to last me a lifetime and a half.

STANCEAUTOMAG|MERRICK HARDING

Jacob
1990 Nissan r32 GT-R

Instagram: @quickzillaz
Photographer: @merrick_media

Author: Merrick Harding

I grew up in Las Vegas NV and I've been into cars for as long as I can remember. My mother was the one that got me into cars, most of my childhood I sat in the garage and watched her fully rebuild a 1969 Pontiac Firebird so I think it started from there.

I have a 1990 Nissan Skyline GTR, I got it completely stock and it was painted in Kl0- spark silver metallic and had 200k kilometres.

A lot has been done to it recently including a full HKS group A livery and a full single turbo conversion. The car makes 409 horsepower on 10psi of boost which is less than stock.

I chose this car cause I had a vision of what I wanted to do with it, I wanted something unique that would turn heads and I wanted to make it iconic. The livery definitely makes the car unique, it took weeks of searching images and trying to get it exactly to the original.

It also has green-tinted headlights to match the original car it's based on. Most People would stray away from the livery and light but I thought it was right down my alley.

The car is not finished, I plan on doing a full engine build and gutting the entire interior at some point. Then painting the entire chassis Nismo white.

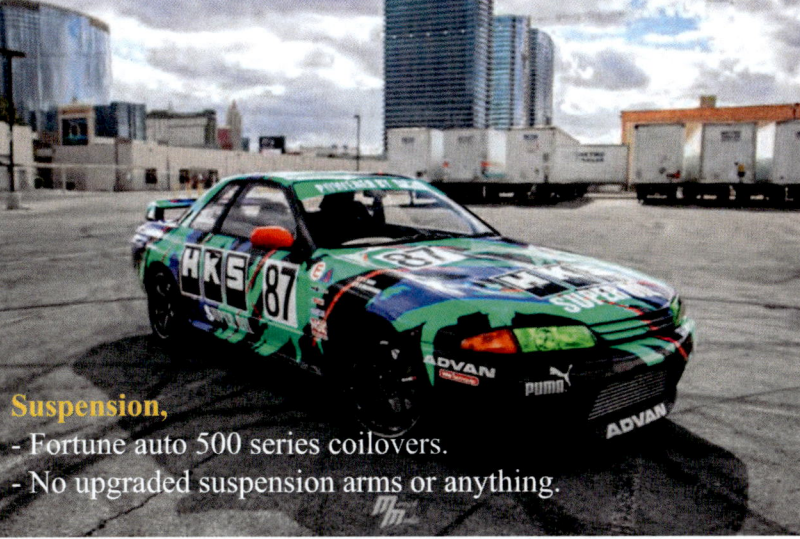

Wheels,
- Omori spec Nismo LMGT4's
- Yokohama Advan A052 tires, 255's all around

Engine
- Garrett gtx3582R gen 2 turbo,
- Doc race Exhaust manifold,
- Custom fabbed downpipe,
- Full Greddy intercooler and intercooler piping,
- HKS cams and cam gears,
- HKS fuel rail with 1050cc Injectors,
- Custom polished intake manifold,
- Mishimoto radiator,
- Radium catch cans

Exterior
- Full HKS livery and Green tinted headlights with a powered HKS banner.

Interior is stock besides an LCD screen that was installed and a vertex steering wheel. I do have two Bride x vertex carbon racing seats but they are not installed yet.

The drive train is stock but the car still has the original Hicas system.

Suspension,
- Fortune auto 500 series coilovers.
- No upgraded suspension arms or anything.

Future plans,
- Full HKS complete engine,
- Complete custom roll cage and dash,
- Complete fuel system,
- OS giken sequential trans,
- Fully painted chassis in white.

Mention @kaijumotorsports as a mechanic, best in Vegas
Mention @incognitowrapslv for the wrap job

Richard Saenz
1989 Nissan Skyline R32 Gtst-t

Instagram: @dat1r32
Photographer: @ab.photomedia

Author: Arryn Bradley

I'm thirty years old and I'm from Corpus Christi, Texas. What first piqued my interest in cars was the Power Wheels Jeep my dad bought me as a kid. However, my interest turned to tuners when I was roughly seven or eight. I remember my parents driving past CiCi's Pizza on the weekends and all the OG's would be meeting up there.

I drive a 1989 Nissan Skyline GTS-T and yes, I know it's not a GTR but I went with the GTS-T because I wanted a moon roof.

I'm sure everyone assumes that I got this car because of Paul Walker and although that would be a safe assumption, the main reason is that as a kid I took a specific Hot Wheels with me EVERYWHERE and I would always tell myself that one day I would get one, and as you guessed it, it was a Skyline.

What makes my car unique among others is its authentic Pandem widebody kit. It's definitely still a work in progress but my next mod is an RB26 motor swap with a single turbo.

I'd like to say that once the motor is done that it's the last thing for the car but, as all car enthusiasts know we're never truly done.

I'd like to leave off by giving a huge thank you to the following people: my family for all their love and support. My buddy Erick who makes sure I never cut corners. Ahmed at Yoson Unlimited, Andres at All Aspects, Eric at Full Lock Collective, Alex at Tuner Goods, Yuya at Avant Garde Wheels, Seth at Dress up bolts, and anyone else who's helped and pushed me along the way, Thank you all.

Sponsors:
@agwheels
@ae_threads
@fulllockcollective
@imperialmats
@dressupbolts

Wheels/Tires:
- Avant-Garde SR8
- 18x10 -50
- 18x12 -38

Toyo R888r
- F: 235/40/18
- R: 295/30/18

Exterior:
- Seibon DVII Carbon hood
- Authentic Pandem R32 Skyline Kit
- Custom Carbon Fiber R32 Pandem Spoiler
- Pandem S15 front splitter

Suspension:
- BC Br Extreme Low Coilovers w/Swift Spring
- Voodoo13 Hard Clear rear toe arms
- Voodoo13 Hard Clear rear traction arms
- Voodoo13 Hard Clear rear camber arms
- Voodoo13 eccentric lockout kit
- Voodoo13 Front Caster Arm
- GKtech Front Upper Camber Arms
- ABS delete kit
- Power HICAS delete
- Front Strut Bar

Performance:
- Apexi 503-N101 Power Intake
- Tomei Dump Tube
- Apexi Downpipe
- Tomei Titanium Cat Delete
- Tomei Titanium Catback Exhaust
- Greddy Trust Intercooler

Interior:
- Custom suede shifter/ebrake boots
- Bloc racing limited 24ct gold shift knob
- LED bulb swapped interior
- Takata Racing Asm Harness
- Works Bell Quick Release
- Works Bell short Hub
- Vertex "King of Vertex" Suede wheel
- Bride/Vertex Fixed back Seats
- Suede Wrapped Roof
- Bride Interior Floor Mats

Audio:
- Sony XAV-7000 double din
- Arc Audio 6x5 602 Door Speakers
- Arc Audio X2 10" Subwoofer
- Arc Audio X2 1100.5 Amplifier
- Custom Ported Subwoofer Box
- Sound Shield sound deadening: Full vehicle

Steve Beefy Botham
Mitsubishi Evo 9 GT

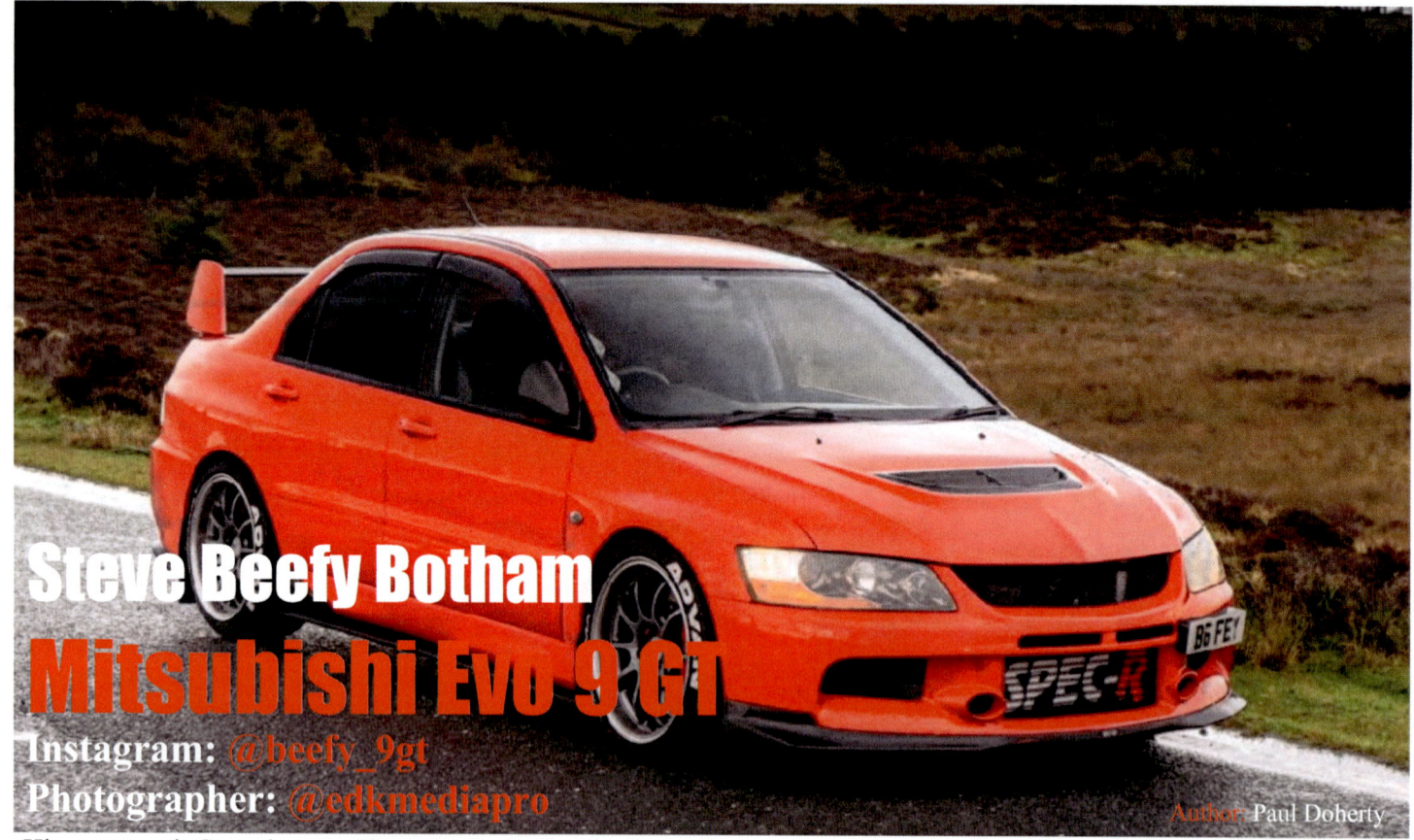

Instagram: @beefy_9gt
Photographer: @edkmediapro

Author: Paul Doherty

Hi, my name is Steve but most know me as beefy, I've been a petrol head for as long as I can remember as growing up my old man had nice cars like Xr2i's, Rs Cosworth's and sports bikes so if I wasn't around his bikes and cars we were sat inside watching racing on TV.

Growing up the dream was always a Lamborghini Countach or the Ferrari F40 but that was never going to happen. As I passed my test I went through a lot of cars from nova's to Rs turbo's and to be fair I'm an old Ford guy at heart, so I've had my fair share of xr2's and Rs turbos. The Rs turbo was the last car before I turned Jap.

My best friend had already turned to Jap as he had brought a skyline and I just knew the jap's were light years ahead, but for me, it had to be an Evo as they looked better in my eyes, the first Evo I brought was an Evo 6 and it was a fantastic car. I did a few small mods to this including a remap. After a couple of years, I traded it in for an Evo 8 mrfq340 in gunmetal grey. I loved the car and used it for a few years as a daily car.

For personal reasons, the car had to go and many other makes of cars were tried but nothing came close to an Evo so I knew one day I would be back in one. That day came and I knew it had to be a red or white Evo 9gt. It had to be the GT model as it was basically an Rs drive train (stronger) with all the creature comforts as an MR like air-con and electric windows.

The car was purchased from a guy in Preston after I persuaded him to sell it to me. The car hadn't been imported long so I knew it should be a clean car and clean it was, with not even a speck of rust on it, even on the underside!

The first job was to put my private plate on it and some small carbon mirrors which I had saved from my old Evo. Then some more gauges and to change the wheels for some black multi-spoke ones. Not long after that, it was time for some carbon rear badges, carbon side skirts, carbon spats, carbon rear bumper extensions, carbon bonnet vent, carbon bonnet lifters and some USDM rear lights. Soon after came an AMS spark plug cover and a rear vortex.

It was used for going to the odd car meet and car show but I knew I needed to not use it in winter to keep the salt away from it and to stop any sign of rot appearing on it so a 106 Gti was purchased for a daily. Later a full Tomei titanium exhaust was fitted alongside a battery relocation to the boot and a spec-r intercooler and pipework including a tial BOV, after changing them I knew it would need a remap so down to London it went to get it mapped which made a healthy 400/400.

After this, I turned my attention to the suspension and went for a set of Ohlins which made night and day difference. This is how it was left for a while as I turned to learn how to detail and make carbon parts. When I decided to kick off modding it again I started with a fresh set of wheels from Japan and I believe they are the only set on an Evo still to date in the UK. They are Yokohama Advan racing rz-df.

These were fitted with some Yokohama Advan tyres with some tyre stickers from tyre stickers in the USA, just to make them a bit more different, accompanied with a set of Ralliart mud flaps. This made the brakes look tatty so it was time to sort them out with a set of alcons for both the front and rear. I changed the stick on number plate for a Jap sized plate with a custom carbon plate holder. I used the car for a few shows and a trip to the Evo triangle.

For a while the colour had been bugging me as even though it was immaculate the paint had been ruined by someone in Japan lacquering the car and getting moisture in with it so it gave it a slight Pearl look and not the proper OEM colour it should be. So after a lot of visits to numerous places across England I settled for Steve at Steve smart repairs in Stoke-on-Trent, who did an amazing job on it! With the new paint, it was time for some new front lights to keep it looking brand new.

This year I thought the gauges were looking dated, so I decided to go digital so all of the gauges and even the OEM clusters were removed and replaced with a syvecs s7 ECU and an aim Strada dash display. As well as this the guys at GR Performance also fitted a Rexspeed rear carbon diffuser and also remapped it.

This is where I'm now at with the car and now all the safety side of things are done on the car it's now to look into upping the power! Roll on next year for some shows so I can get out in it and use it some more!

Spec list:

Interior;
- Standard GT interior
- Aim Strada dash
- Battery relocated to the boot
- Fire extinguisher in the boot

Exterior;
- Full OEM spray job including on shuts
- USDM rear lights
- New front MR lights
- Smoked side repeaters
- Carbon vortex
- Rexspeed carbon diffuser
- Rexspeed carbon bumper extensions
- Carbon side skirts
- Carbon small mirrors
- Carbon Ralliart front splitter
- Tomei ti exhaust and decat
- Tomei turbo elbow and downpipe
- Spec-r intercooler and pipework
- 18" avan Rz-df dished wheels
- Alcon front and back brake set up
- Genuine Mitsubishi wind deflectors
- Ohlins suspension

Engine;
- Syvecs s7
- Tomei Ti exhaust
- Spec-r intercooler and pipework
- K&n large air filter
- Reworked 71 series turbo
- 3 port solenoid
- Uprated fuel pump
- Uprated fuel rail
- Uprated fuel regulator

Credit where credit is due to;
Pete from @specralloy
Ross Walker from @rosssport
Steve and the guys at Steve's smart repairs,
Garry and James at GR Rerformance for the last finishing touches to get it where it is to date.

Jay Lyons
1994 Acura NSX

Instagram: @imjaylyons and @the.real.ams
YouTube: I'm Jay Lyons

Author: Carla De Freitas

I'm 35, from Philadelphia and I've been building cars since I was 15. I've built countless cars, I am on a quest to become known as one of America's best builders.

I own a shop called AMS Auto Moto Specialist's (@the.real.ams). In terms of what services we provide, let's say, we build custom cars and work on absolutely anything, I started from nothing and built it into a very reputable company, We have even built pro athletes and celebs.

My obsession for the NSX all started at age 11 when I was at a car show and saw an NSX for the very first time! I have been obsessed ever since. I even had a 5 gallon water jug that said "NSX Fund" on the front, written on a piece of duct tape, from the time I was about 17!

I had saved up enough money to buy the car about 6 times before I actually used the money to purchase one. Other priorities kept coming up like, house, renovation's, engagement, wedding, starting my business etc. When I was finally ready to buy an NSX I found one in Las Vegas. The deal fell through at the last minute and I must admit I was super upset! I had been trying to buy a red one from a guy in New York for about a month but, he had promised the car to someone else! Gutting I know.

One night I came home to a text message at 8:30pm saying
"IF YOU STILL WANT THE CAR I'LL SELL IT TO YOU BUT, IT HAS TO BE TODAY."
I had just got home from a long day and I could not miss the opportunity so I drove to get the car with some friends and was on my way home with it by 2am!

It took me about 3 years to complete the work we have done on the NSX and in terms of modifications, the list is as follows:-

Suspension:
This setup is pretty unique. I am running KW V3 coil overs with an air cup kit. The air suspension is activated by a switch that I built into the dummy pedal next to the clutch. So to lift the car you push the dummy pedal, and then again to lower the car. It's hands free and lifts the car by 3-4 inches. Aside from that I replaced the basic wear and tear items like control arms, axles, wheel hub bearings.

Exterior:
- Fully disassembled and painted the car;
- Wider front fenders;
- NA2 valance kit, with a wings west front lip;
- Replaced the front windshield;
- JDM headlights and led bulbs;

The hood is full Carbon fibre which I painted red, but left the vents carbon;

The paint job is what is referred to as a "Concourse Level" paint job Meaning it is extremely high quality and shows no flaws or texture. It's usually one of the first things people notice when they see the car;

Wheels
- SSR Agle Strusse.
- 18x9 in the front
- 19x10.5 rear.

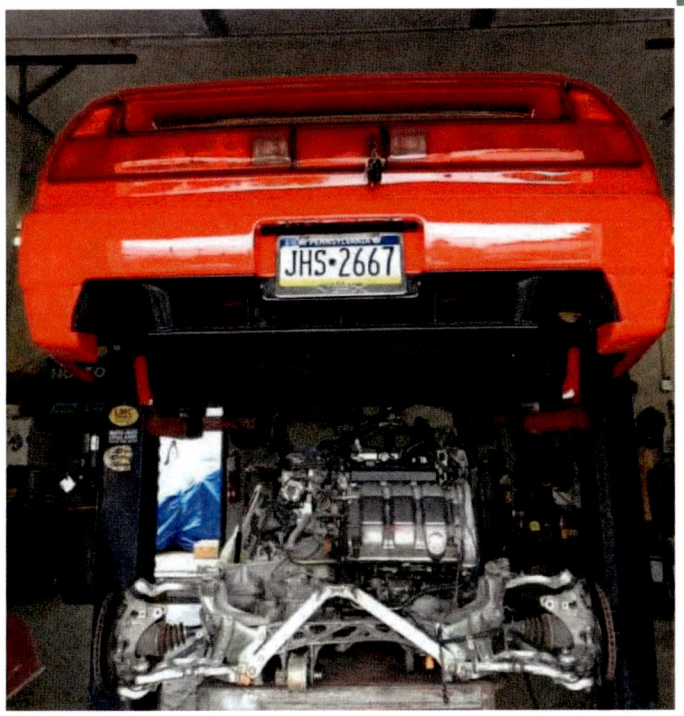

Engine:
The engine is stock. I removed it and resealed it. Spruced it up with some red powder coat and cleaning. I built a supercharger system using a kit that came off of my mustang.

It's a Pro Charger P1SC. It's all custom; nobody sells a kit for the NSX. I mounted a vibrant heat exchanger behind the front bumper, and plumbed it to an air to water intercooler mounted to the air intake in the engine bay, and fluid is cycled through a Shelby GT500 intercooler pump.

I built a coolant reservoir to fit in the engine bay, we upgraded the fuel system and Injectors and tuned the car on an AEM stand-alone. We built the exhaust system from scratch, using a kit we ordered for a v6 mustang from Roush Performance. They wouldn't sell me just the mufflers so I had to do it that way.

I have started to attend car shows/competition's this year however, I have not yet competed yet. This year I was invited to many really big shows for a VIP spot at 'Tuner Evolution', 'Elite Tuner' and 'Clean Culture'.

I have attended a few local meets this year, to be quite honest, I enjoy meets more than shows as I think they are more of a hangout. At shows I feel like I have to stay with my car constantly and explain all the work that has been done. The only reason as to why I have not gone to any shows in the past is purely because; I just did not have the time! I have had to work crazy hours to get the shop to the point it's currently at. I have just started a YouTube channel and I am going to start posting, promoting and hit shows like crazy!

Watch this space… My main goal is to market my company and cars like crazy this coming summer.

Thank you for your time in reading my article, don't forget to give us a follow on Instagram and subscribe to my YouTube channel for some more content.

Interior:
I had my upholstery guy redo the entire interior using high grade Italian leather and alcantera. The seats, headliner, and door cards are all custom made. We made insert panels for the headliner which give it an awesome look.

Also, I built a centre console from fiberglass which houses an 8" sub-woofer. You can't tell there is a sub in there, it looks like it's supposed to be there but it kicks out some great sound.

My current car collection of fully built cars-

- 1993 Mustang Cobra 347 with nitrous
- 1992 Mustang LX 5.0 37k miles
- 1982 Buick Regal Low rider with hydraulics. 50k original miles
- 1996 Chevy Impala SS
- 1991 Honda CRX 700hp custom steel wide body
- 1968 Mustang Pro Touring Car
- 1992 Infiniti M30 Convertible
- 2007 Saleen S331 Supercharged
- 2015 Cadillac Escalade on 26's
- 1990 F150 low rider on white walls

Rebecca Sweet
Lexus IS200

Instagram: @bex_lex
Photographer F/B: SCE Photography

Author: Paul Doherty

I'm a hairdresser in Lymington, I live in Southampton with my partner Peter Robins and my little dog Purdy.

I have always liked cars due to my dad being a banger racer at matchams and other places. He is also a car mechanic, I used to go to work with him when I was a child and banger racing too.

Also due to my brother in law (Elvin Lake) who is also into cars and has had quite a few modified cars over the years, we go to shows together and also with a lot of his friends and my friends too.

Since I passed my test 4 years ago I have become more into cars and attending car shows and meets all over the place.

I go to Silverstone, Beaulieu Motor Museum, Goodwood, Castle Combe, places like that. I also attend little car meets in the area I live in and other places like Bournemouth, Poole, London, Portsmouth, Hedge End etc.

Since owning the Lexus I have been brought more into the car scene due to her being the only 1 on throttle bodies.

The people at shows who have seen this car on ITB'S have gone mad whether they own a Lexus or not! Everyone loved her and since posting her up on my Instagram @bex_lex she has had a lot of interest even from people over in America!

I've had all sorts of messages asking about the car and the mods etc. These cars are so comfy to drive it's unreal, also a benefit is the heated seats for the winter as I'm always cold Also the Lexus are great drift cars, very easy to drift and great fun to drive.

Also people with this type of car tend to turbo or supercharge them but I wanted to be different and put Individual Throttle Bodies on.

Here is the Spec of the car:

- Throttle bodies
- Omex ecu
- Vibratechnic raving mounts
- HSD dual tech coilovers
- Cobra sport exhaust (resonated)
- Dotz wheels (custom painted)
- Stripped out rear
- Custom made bonnet
- Window tints
- TRD front lip and skirts
- TTE rear lip
- Halo headlights
- Tinted front and rear lights
- Oil and power steering radiators
- Custom manifold

For the car to look the way it does and have all mods done has been by me and my partner who is an auto electrician and mechanic and also has a modified car, we've also had a few companies to help, which are.

Phoenix Automotive Technologies in Verwood, to tune the car including map which is unknown due to more mods being done so she has got to go back for a remap and getting her running.

Read Performance in New Milton to modify the bonnet which he made the scoop all by hand!

I have owned 2 cars before the Lexus is200 they were, Fiat Cinquecento in black not yellow like the car from the inbetweeners, the other car was a Suzuki Swift 2002 model with a custom made stainless steel exhaust done by Read Performance and lowered on springs.

I am planning to do more mods to the car like possibly getting cams made or even change the engine to a LS from GM. No one has ever done this before so again unique to me!

I have a car group of my own called Mofo Customs and we sometimes do little meets down Portsdown hill while having a burger from Monster Micks Burger Van and sometimes Hedge End and South Sea. We are on Facebook and Instagram so check us out.

My alternative dream car is a Nissan GTR R35! They are beautiful to look at and they sound beautiful. The only thing I would change on 1 of them cars is going from automatic gearbox to manual, I love driving manual cars, makes it more fun and exciting and the colour has to either be black or white, those are my favourite car colours hence the black Lexus

Shantih Beadnell
Toyota GT86 D-S4

Instagram: @duckyy_17.
Photographer: @s.beadnell_photography

Author: Paul Doherty

I'm 24 from Manchester and work in adult social care! Like to take the occasional photo (@s.beadnell_photography) I'm currently driving a pearl white Toyota GT86 D-4S (if we want to be specific!) It's factory-fitted with the naturally aspirated 2 litres Subaru Boxer engine.

Mods:
Wrapped orange gloss roof by @vinylgraphics_evanshalshaw after winning it in a Facebook give away!
40mm @eibach_world lowering springs which were kindly fitted for me by a fellow car buddy @f8ngy
@remark_exhaust backbox/silencer delete with 4.5-inch tips. Fitted by a local garage
Valenti rear lights which were already upgraded on the car at purchase.

Following mods fitted at home:
@mishimoto performance air intake
@maxtondesign front splitter with rod support
@gramsstyling BGW.
@japanracingwheels (JR18. 18x8.5 et35) covered with Uni-royal rain sport 3 tyres (225/40/18)
@getnrg short hub and @kode_shop steering wheel custom painted white with gold spokes.
@wearelikewise 'The Neil Diamond' gear knob in 'Tiffany and Hoe'
Interior and engine bay bits sprayed in orange and teal with gold sparkle.
A bunch of stickers mostly supplied by my sponsor @unidentified_graphics (use code DUCKY2020 in your message to them for a discount!)

Misc items;
- Side window louvres in gloss black.
- Rear bumper spats.
- Carbon headlight surrounds.
- Interior footwell lights.
- Private plate.

I will try and attempt various things in my own car with the help of @orange_zmcgee. There's no better feeling than achieving something yourself - the only problem is you then don't want to stop and that's when things get expensive!

Previous cars:
Got my first car when I was 19 - my 1.4 Citroën C2. I loved it but quickly upgraded. That car introduced me to the car scene and I'm still friends with plenty of the C2 owners I met back then! I upgraded to a Mercedes A200 AMG Sport (no - not the one with the Renault engine!) I didn't really do much. Just fitted a carbon wing (not the A45 replica) and added some orange trim here and there.

I bought a Mk2 MX5 California. These are a limited edition and hard to find now! This car introduced me to real modifications (intakes, coilovers, wheels, exhaust etc.) we attended a number of shows and I was at my happiest driving it! Sadly, going to work one day a white van decided to jump his filter and we crashed!

The car was later sold to someone who will restore it and love it as I did! The 86 isn't yet finished but we've come a long way! I'm after some coilovers next. Some side skirts, upgraded headlights and to sort a few other visual modifications! Is a modified car ever really finished though..?

@trueaddictionuk is my real car family. I've been with them from the start and I couldn't wish for a better set of friends! They can be found on Facebook and Instagram and at every major car show! We have a store too so drop me a message if you want a discount!
www.trueaddictionuk.co.uk

Thanks to @mirrorimagecarcare for making amazing car cleaning products which keep my car gleaming! A quick shout out to these groups who also have a great culture: @exclusivejdm @driftkingzcarclub and @extremebhp
Thanks to @24sevenphotography for one of the photos used!

I mainly attend shows, major ones such as Japfest, Japshow, Modified Nationals, Fast Show, Trax (both of them), FittedUK and Ultimate Stance. Due to the location of most shows, me and @orange_zmcgee are usually up at 3 am getting ready to travel on show day! My dream car, They're all Jap! A 1997 Nissan 180SX, or a 1995 Honda Nsx. However, I'd love a clean, rust-free MK1 MX5 California #BringBackPopUpLights!
Oh... And an RX7. Maybe I'm just being greedy now!

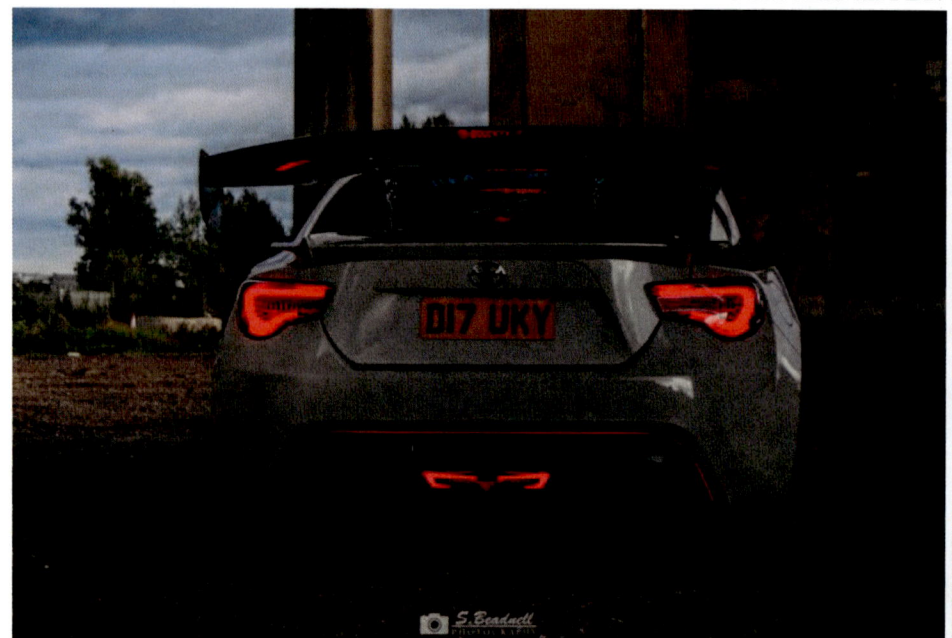

Andrew Williams
R34 Super widebody Skyline

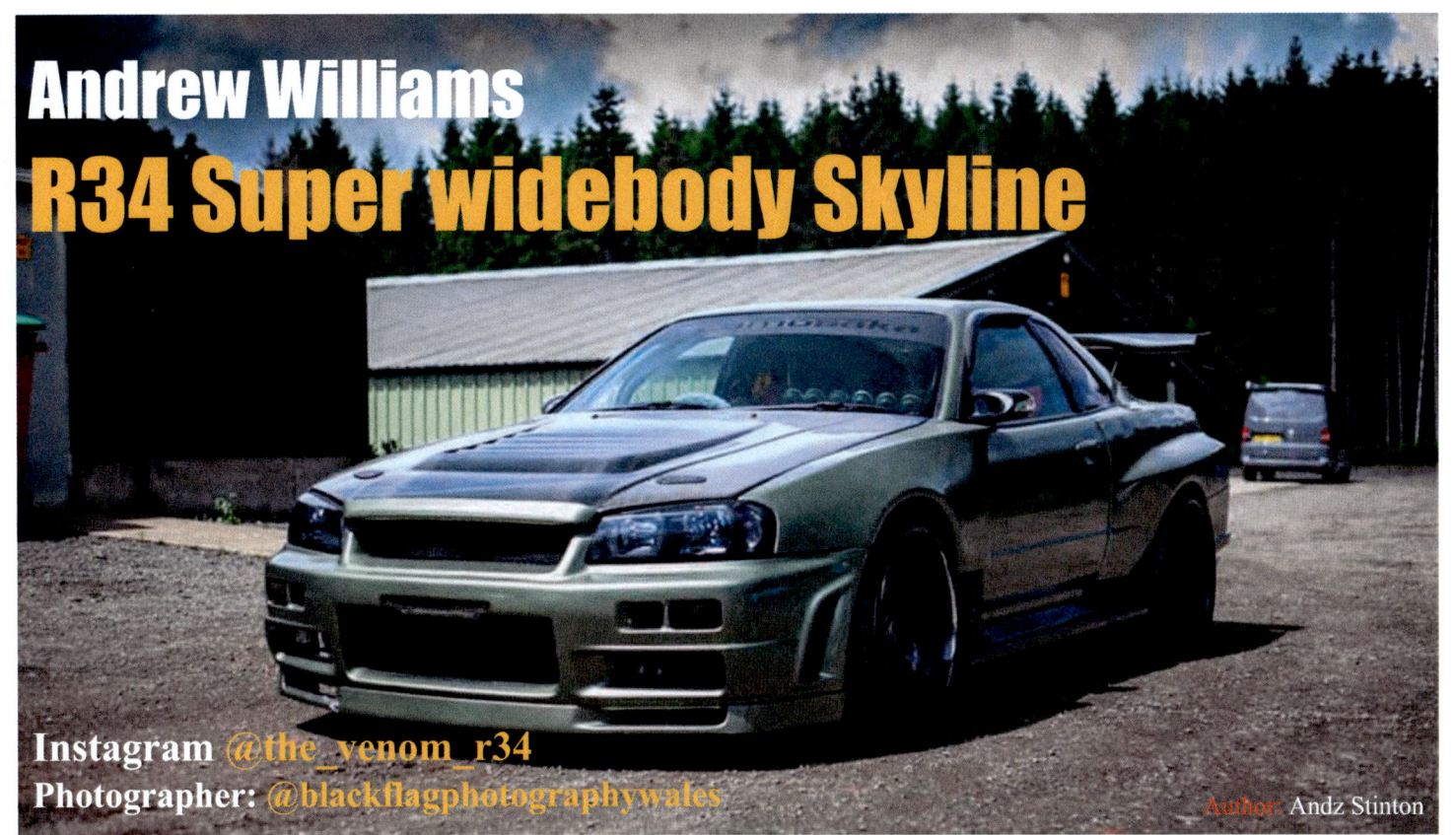

Instagram @the_venom_r34
Photographer: @blackflagphotographywales

Author: Andz Stinton

I'm 42 years old and I live in Port Talbot, South Wales. I'm unable to work due to ill health.

At 17 I got my licence and my first car was 1.8 injection mk2 cavalier, at this time I worked in a local sports centre and I met a guy by the name of John Powell who drove an absolutely beautiful mk4 escort van with a full Rs body kit and a Rs turbo engine, we became good friends and before I knew it I was looking at my first set of alloy wheels.

So it was the influence of John and his van that gave me the bug that would cost me thousands over the years.

I also grew up in an environment where my parents loved their cars, they mainly had little MG sports cars and one car that really sticks in my memory is my father's bright orange Cortina 2200e which my father put a bubble kit on, chrome wheels and radial tyres and even today in their late 70's they are still in to cars.

Currently I own an R34 super widebody Skyline that's known as Venom. I imported the car via a company called @japwestmods 5 years ago and when it arrived in the country it was all black and now its millennium jade.

The car started off as a black completely stock R34 GTT auto and a company called Final Konnexion bought the vehicle to build it as a demo car for their company and made its debut at Tokyo Auto Salon.

They completely changed the look of the car, they replaced the rear quarters and wings with custom carbon fiber over fenders.

They created a Frankenstein bumper by blending an east bear and s-tune bumper together to compensate for the width on the body kit that was fitted, slammed it with Tein coil overs and custom made 20inch AME shallen wheels which were originally 9.5j front and 10.5j rear but ended up being 10.5j front and 11.5j rear.

The final touch was wrapping the car gloss white.

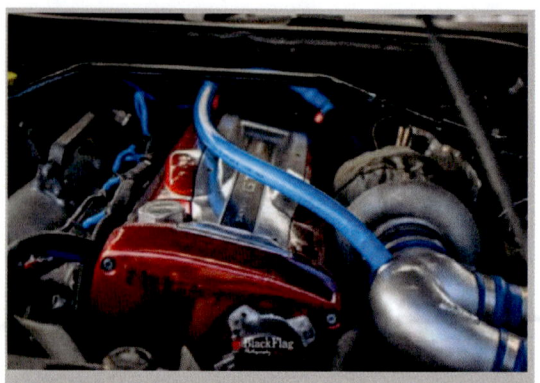

Specs List
Engine

- Brian Crower 2.85 stroker kit
- Brian Crower 87.5 Forge Pistons
- Brian Crower 4.782" 625+ connecting rods
- Brian Crower forged 79mm Crankshaft
- Brian Crower Stage 4 Camshafts
- Brian Crower valve springs
- Brian Crower titanium Retainers
- Brian Crower head gasket
- Legalis Super R Ported and Polished Head
- Greddy T88r-33D turbo
- Greddy external wastegate
- Screamer pipe
- 4" Custom downpipe
- Fujitsubo Exhaust System
- Twin z32 Maf
- Twin RamAir induction kits
- Apexi Stainless Turbo intake
- NKGR Plugs
- OEM coil packs
- Mobile 3000 10/40 semi synthetic race oil
- HKS high flow oil filter
- Stainless Sump Guard
- 1200cc injectors
- 7th injector regulator
- 5bar FPR
- Walbro Fuel pump
- Nismo 35L fuel tank
- HPI inlet
- 3.5" Steel hard pipes
- 5.5" Blitz Front Mount Intercooler
- Greddy Oil Cooler
- Evolve ally rad
- Twin cooling fans
- Apexi FC Ecu
- Greddy boost controller

Joy's of importing a car, the car didn't come with much paper work and what I did have was all in Japanese. I've done a lot of research on the car to find out who did what and when however I was unable to find out who completed the engine conversion. I'm assuming that the build had something to do with Brain Crower as every part of the engines intenernal are BC.

The result of all the engine work that's been carried out is 726bhp on low boost and over 900bhp on high boost When the car arrived in the UK, I purchased a set of red type R seats, painted the car millennium jade, changed the wheels and fitted a top secret spoiler. Here is Venoms current.

Besides the fact it's an R34 skyline which you don't see many of, all my modifications are custom and are a 'one off'. One thing I know for sure, my car can never be replicated. I'm in the process of further modifying the rear suspension but I'm basically where I want to be with this car, when I met my wife 10 years ago I said my dream would be to own a R34 and my dream came true in 2015.

Any detailing work I need completing that I can't do myself, Joseph Roberts at JR Detailed, Treorchy, hooks me up. My paint work is done by Matthew at Paint by Sanders, Neath, South Wales and so far all mechanical work that's been needed has only been service and maintenance so that has been completed by friends and family. Also a buddy of mine who helped me get venom in to the country, getting its through its first MOT and looking after the car whilst it was registered for UK ROADS, Matt Kayo Kervin, he's helped me so much over the years and I will forever be grateful for everything he has done and no doubt will do in the future.

Running Gear
- Custom 1 off built 5speed manual
- R34 GTT Bell housing
- Custom top secret final drive
- Nismo short shifter
- 6Puk Nismo clutch
- Nismo 2 way LSD
- Brembo 330 4pot front calipers
- Brembo 330 2pot rear calipers
- EBC Disks and pads all round

Suspension
- Tein Coilovers
- Cusco chassis brace
- Trust upper strut brace
- Trust rear strut brace
- Ally lower arms
- Custom adjustable steering arms
- 40mm front and rear Anti-roll bars
- Full polyurethane Bush conversion

Wheels
ROTA GTR-D
Front 18x10.5   245/40/18
Rear 18x12.5   295/30/18

Exterior
- OEM Millennium Jade
- 1 off Carbon Super wide body built by Apache racing for final konnexion.
- 1 off carbon side skirts
- 1 off carbon triple winglets
- Carbon boot lip spoiler
- Z tune Carbon bonnet
- Carbon ganador wing mirrors
- Full carbon Top Secret Spoiler
- Bonnet lip extension
- East bear bumper modified to fit
- Limo tint rear glass
- Smoked xenon headlights
- Smoked indicators
- LED Nismo rear lights
- F1 style repeaters

Interior
- Full Cusco Roll cage
- RECARO Red Reclining seats
- Sparco Subframes
- 5pc tailored mat set
- Sparco harness pads
- Nismo gear knob
- Centre console custom painted Nismo red / Metallic
- GTR pedals
- KODE steering wheel
- D1 snap off boss
- 6x defi gauges
- Boost
- Oil pressure
- Oil temperature
- Fuel pressure
- Water temperature
- Exhaust temperature
- All recordable with playback
- Sony Double din head unit
- CD / Mp3 / Bluetooth / DR
- 2 x 10" in-phase Subwoofer
- 1800w 4channel amplifier
- Private plate R28 VNM
- (Rb28 venom)

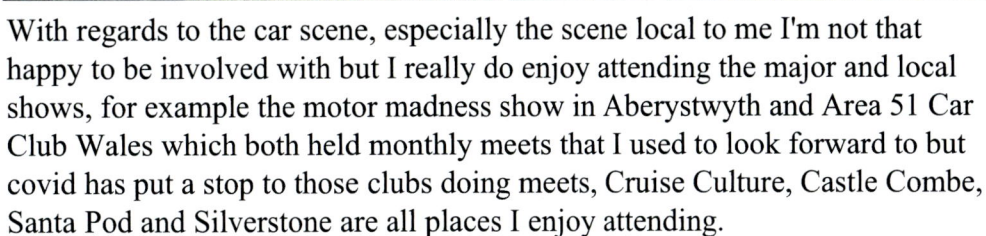

With regards to the car scene, especially the scene local to me I'm not that happy to be involved with but I really do enjoy attending the major and local shows, for example the motor madness show in Aberystwyth and Area 51 Car Club Wales which both held monthly meets that I used to look forward to but covid has put a stop to those clubs doing meets, Cruise Culture, Castle Combe, Santa Pod and Silverstone are all places I enjoy attending.

I help run @Area51CarClubwales alongside my wife. It's a club where I can really be myself, be around people of similar age to myself and most importantly be around like minded people. I previously attended shows with Superior Rides, they are a great bunch and are so welcoming. I highly recommend them both.

Christina Williams
Nissan 350z - Ned the Zed
Instagram: @sprouty92

Author: Andz Stinton

I'm 28 years old and I'm from Port Talbot, South Wales,. I'm unemployed due to being registered as a full time carer to my beautiful disabled daughter however I did complete Btec Level 3 in Motor Vehicle in Tycoch college before my daughters disability got to the point where it became impractical and impossible for me to return to work. I have to admit I wasn't really into cars when I was a kid, I was all about 2 wheels instead of 4.

Every Sunday without fail me and my amazing step mum would jump in the car and take a trip to the local Yamaha dealership and we would spend a good 2 hours there looking at the bikes. I'll never forget the day my dad gave me food poisoning, my stepmother took me for our usual Sunday outing however I spewed all over a brand new R1 and a little scooter leaving my stepmother in an awful position of cleaning up my spew whilst she has a horrifically weak stomach herself. I'll never forget or live that day down!

What really sparked my interest in cars was my partner, when I first met him I had not long passed my test and was in the process of saving for a car. I was going to be sensible and get a little run around to get me back and forth work, he had different ideas. When I had around £500 saved we started having a look, we came across a bright orange Micra k11 that had been converted from a 1L to a 1.3 turbo.

It was proper Max power style, ridiculous bumpers, side skirts, blacked out windows and lights, oh and bright orange bucket seats.

That was it, I was in love. Every day I was off I was cleaning the car or fiddling. But one day it started misfiring and I panicked like hell as I didn't know what was going on, that's when my partner said to me 'right you can clean a car, now time to learn how to maintain a car' we bought a full service kit and he talked me through each step and at the ripe age of 19 I completed my first service and absolutely I was chuffed with myself.

After my Micra had a 200bhp Ibiza Cupra but it wasn't really for me, I'm a Jap girl, simple as that so Ibiza had to go! I have owned 3 Subaru Impreza Classic wrx and 1 Subaru hatchback wrx. However when my daughter joined an amazing special needs school, I needed to get a diesel as I'm doing 250miles a week just on the school run.

That's when I decided that my Subaru Hatchback needed to go, plus it was ridiculously loud and a lot of the children could cope with the noise. I've always had a soft spot for a 350z so I thought so, I have a sensible daily time for mama to have a 2 seater car and have some fun! So the other half got on the marketplace and he came across my boy. Yes I'm a saddo the name of their car. So everyone meets Ned the Zed! He is a standard colour of solar orange

When it comes to mechanical work that I can't complete myself or my buddy Martin then Rhodri in Dave Coe located Gorseinon, South Wales is my main man, even though my car is a standard colour for any of my painting needs I go to Matthew at Paint by Sanders, Neath, South Wales and when I'm feeling lazy or I haven't got the time to give the car a detail Joseph Roberts at @JR_Detailed, Treorchy, South Wales is the guy I turn too. All very talented men who are very trustworthy.

Over the winter I want to Retrim the interior roof and put lights in the liner, I know my daughter will just adore it, she loves going in the 'orange car' and begs to go for a spin every weekend so I think she will get a right kick from the lights.

Apart from that there isn't much that I want to do to the car apart from maintenance as I love the car as it is.
I do have a goal, I doubt it's achievable however a girl can dream. I would love to have an Nissan Skyline GTR R29, one of the most beautiful skylines ever created!

Unfortunately I have to admit I am not a fan of the car scene, especially over the last few years. People always have something negative to say about other people or what they do and I'm not about that. 7 years ago I was part of a club that the Admins didn't want to be a part of anymore so I took over, if I'm honest it's the best thing I've ever done.

Area 51 Car Club Wales

Spec List:-
- K&N Air filters,
- Stillen gen 3 induction kit,
- Ark performance grip stainless steel twin exit exhaust,
- Air horns,
- Front upper strut brace,
- Nissan skyline r35 carbon vents fitted to bonnet,
- Nismo v3 front bumper,
- Canards on front bumper x4,
- Eyebrows on headlights,
- Sun strip,
- Side window louvres,
- Nismo side skirts,
- Carbon side skirt rear extension blades,
- Rear tinted window in dark smoke,
- Charge speed rear bumper,
- Smoked side repeaters,
- Carbon fiber rear diffuser on bumper,
- Ducktail spoiler,
- Japspeed wing rear spoiler mounted to duck tail,
- 19 inch calibre wheels 8.5 front, 9.5 rear, powder coated in white,
- TGR wheel nuts,
- HKS brake lines
- Tein super street lowering springs,
- Hitch hiker's 24mm front and rear anti roll bars
- Kenwood double din head unit,
- Pioneer under seat subwoofer
- Sparco bucket seat,
- D1 slim line boss kit,
- Sparco extreme control deep dish steering wheel.

Louis Archbold
1993 Skyline r32
Instagram: @r32_archie

Author: Paul Doherty

I'm 27. From Suffolk and a Bench Joiner, so basically make fancy stuff out of timber and that's what funds my car addiction. Everything car wise I've done I've self taught or helped mechanic friends while learning.

I'm an admin of an East Anglia based Jap group called East Coast Japanese, we hold monthly Sunday morning meets with a large turn out of close members with all sorts of Japanese cars from old Jap gems, modern Jap cars or jdm iconic cars.

Going back to the start of my love for cars I started being into the modified car scene as soon as I got on the road when I was 18 in 2011, I was into cars before that but not as much as I am now. The obsession with cars started out like most kids do, watching Fast and Furious and playing racing games. 3 years prior to passing my test I unfortunately lost my dad, but every cloud has a silver lining and he left me a little bit of money for when I turned 18 which helped me pay for my lessons and buy my first car which was a Ford fiesta 1.25. From then I've had 16 cars, some for short periods of times, some which were dailys.

But the main 3 cars which I've loved and built was a s14a which was my pride and joy being my first proper build. After that I had a Jzx100 chaser but sold that and got exported to Germany. With that money I was able to buy 1 of my 2 dream cars, The R32.

I was looking at the GTR R32 but to be honest the plans I had, with how I wanted my skyline to look and be I couldn't get the GTR as its sacrilege to put body kits on them and lower them, the GTR is something you leave besides changing wheels and getting a lot of power out of them. Otherwise you ruin an amazing iconic beautiful car so for this reason I'm glad I went with a GTST m spec.

Funny enough it belonged to a friend who I used to keep joking with to sell it to me, one day out of the blue he messaged me saying would I seriously consider buying it and I jumped at the chance.

A few weeks later and it was done. I had a beautiful gunmetal grey r32 outside my house, I couldn't believe it every time I looked at it or drove it. However, I had bought it just as winter had hit and the salt gritters were out so I had to put it away for a few months which was horrible, buying a dream car but not actually getting to drive it for long due to winter hitting.

Finally, March was here and I was ready to get the car out, now the salt gritters had gone and no more ice but then we all got hit by the pandemic and the country was in lock down. I was still working through the whole thing but not being able to go out after work or weekends gave me the time to start on making the car my own.

The engine conversion was done from when it was still in Japan but was still running stock power. So it had a link g4+ ecu and a few other supporting mods to help get some major power out of the Rb25. So once I did get the car back out I started with removing the current Body kit and fitted and painted the new BN sports kit. Which was a nightmare as anyone who has bought a fiberglass panel or kit knows they always need trimming but I finally got the good fit then prepped and painted it.

Which was a nightmare as anyone who has bought a fiberglass panel or kit knows they always need trimming but I finally got the good fit then prepped and painted it. Next I cracked the wheels off and lowered it, ended up selling the horrible wheels which it was on and got a set of 7twentys but I hit another problem. Wheels hit the front calipers so had to run spacers which meant raising the car up to clear the arch, never felt so sick in my life having to actually raise a car up.

I tried everything to not have to raise it up, like using upper camber adjuster arms, rolling the arches but I had to raise it up for a temporary fix until I get new parts to sort it as I love the wheels too much and want to still run them.

It had the R32 GTR front and rear seats but I wasn't a fan. Too hard and uncomfortable for me so I swapped them out for some Recaros. As you can imagine the car is prone to the police attention. A lot of the time they just ask me about the car and their liking towards it. Then the other times with the police which have been eventful. I still have so much more I want to get done to it, power and looks wise. No car is ever truly done.

Full specs and modifications as follows:
RB25det swapped
Greddy inlet with 80mm throttle.
550cc injectors.
255lt fuel pump.
K and N filter on custom inlet pipework.
Hybrid turbo
FMIC on custom intercooler pipework
Splitfire coil packs
Link g4+ ecu
AM performance downpipe
Silenced decat and stainless exhaust.
Aluminium radiator.
RB20det gearbox with exedy gtr clutch.
Nismo short shift.
Polybush rear subframe
driftworks hicas eliminator.
HSD monopro coilovers.
BN sports body kit
Nardi steering wheel with snap off boss
7twenty style 55 18" 9.5j et15
Recaro reclining bucket seats
Front camber adjusters
Gtr aluminium bonnet (soon to be swapped out)
smoked front lenses

Luke Flear
1.8 UK spec MX5
Project Monstrosity

Author: Andz Stinton

Instagram: @L22_MXV

I'm an Art Teacher and after passing my test and my mum buying me my first car, a 2003 ford fiesta Zetec, I had no intention of modifying it. But one day that all changed and I was approached by the owner of Lincs Fords Group in a Morrisons petrol station and invited to a meet. After that everything was on the cards I had massive plans, order coilovers, purchased wheels and fitted a sub. Starting to learn how to modify it myself with a little guidance from family and friends.

Once I moved to university the love for Japanese cars became apparent while working with a few car lads. So that's when the MX5 came into my life, I bought it off one of the lad's uncles unbeknown to both him and me till I took it to work. So, Chris and Joe, you're both to blame for the MX5 and where it is today!

Once the MX5 was part of my life I started to attend shows with Total-Jap, the car was standard when I purchased it so it has taken a few years to get to where it is today, 5 years so far.

The start of the process wasn't fun, I purchased the car and in the first 500 miles, the head gasket went... so booked it in for the work done as I was at university and too busy, I got it back and it lasted about 200 miles (you could say I don't recommend that garage) so I took the car back and they refused to fix it because it had a cracked the head and that wasn't their fault. So another company, and problem solved? Nope.

Went to another recommended garage for a reconditioned engine because it was easier than sourcing just ahead. So I got the car back and was so happy.

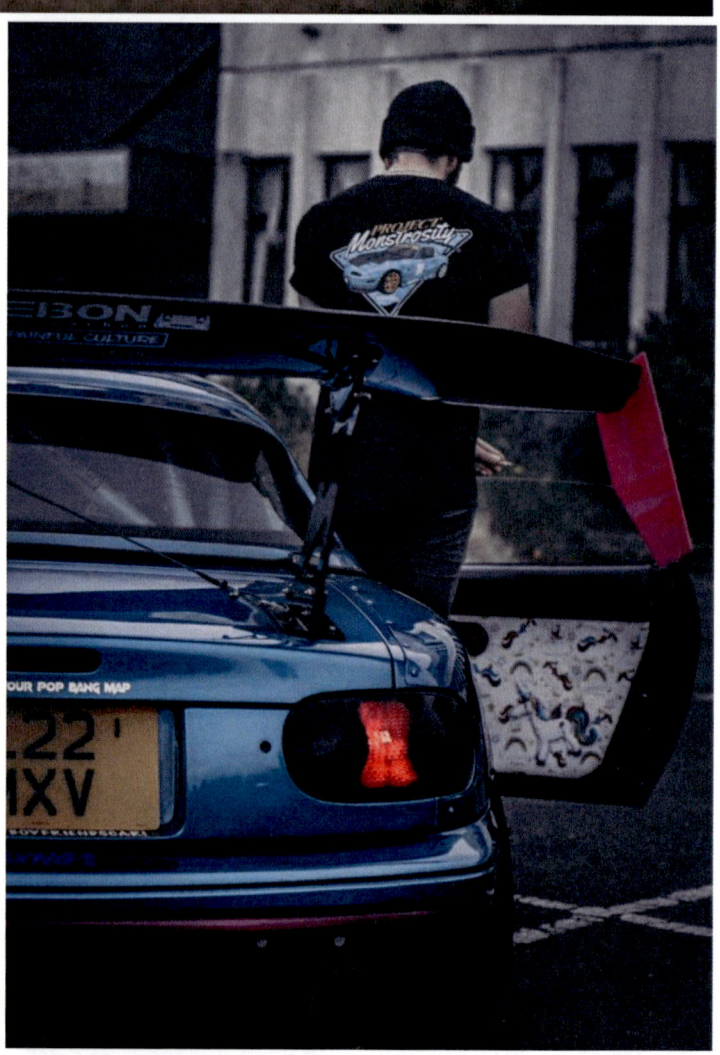

250 miles later one of the brand new timing belt tensioners snapped, so I took it back to the garage and they sorted it at an extra cost to me (luckily only £80). So I thought that was it, all my bad luck was gone? Wrong. About a year later my piston rings gave up so dropped another engine which lasted till I turbo'd the car in April of this year (2020).

So the car itself is a 1.8 UK spec MX5, which I have recently turbo'd. The car has yet to go on a dyno so I'm unsure on an exact power figure, but I'm aiming for 200whp when finished. So the car started standard and I started with the normal stickers and little bits like a stereo, gear knob, air filter etc.

Once I had done all the little bits I bought a set of wheels which I loved then over time started to hate so they had to go, that's when I bought my XXR's that are currently on the car. The Japspeed wing was purchased at some point at the beginning, which I sold, and then ended up buying it back as I missed it that much.

Bodywork wise the car is wide arched on the rear, along with fibreglass vented arches on the front and a carbon Miata AD09 carbon bonnet. The car is painted BMW Atlantis Blue (on a different colour primer to BMW so a slightly different outcome in final colour). Painting the car is the only bit I didn't do, however, I did spend 9 days at the body shop splitting the car, helping prep the car, and then reassembling it.

The car is far from finished, the next plan is to buy front and rear subframes and all the arms then have then powder coated and poly bushed then swap them into the car along with a helical LSD. Then once I've done that it will be getting painted again.

I have done the majority of the work myself apart from painting the car; I have had some help from friends and family. Quick shout out to all the people that have helped me along the way, even if it was just with advice or providing parts etc. There are a few companies who have made it possible for me to build my dream. Green light Insurance being the main one, massive shout out to them, check them out for any insurance needs!

I occasionally attend large shows at Santa Pod Raceway, Silverstone etc, with Total-Jap, however I have had the opportunity to go on trade stands alongside Green light Insurance, which I couldn't turn down. The car has been built purely for my pleasure and I didn't build it to win shows, but it has won a few little events (2nd Best On Stand, Best Interior). I am going to look at running some track days next year but I want the suspension set up sorting first.

'Project Monstrosity'
So 4 engines, and 100 hours of work I'm still going! Don't give up on your dreams, build it for you, not other people... 'The cars we drive say a lot about us' My achievable dream car is a Nissan Laurel C35, I don't know why just been a car I fell in love with and that's never changed if money wasn't a question the Lexus LFA would be in my garage.

Exterior
- XXR 522 (16x8.25 ET2)
- D1 spec tuner nuts
- Ad09 Vented Carbon Bonnet
- Bonnet Pins
- Bilstein Suspension
- Fibreglass vented wings
- Fibreglass rear over arches
- Duce side skirts
- Vented headlight cover
- Raybrig headlight lenses
- CM composite side spats
- Hardtop
- Jass performance TSIs
- GV style front lip
- Luke tow strap (front and rear)
- Quick-release bumper catches
- Skull Fab front jacking bar
- FPM rear jacking bar
- Japspeed BGW (Pink Perspex end plates)
- Grams Styling RX7 rear diffuser
- Front canards
- Project G Hardtop spoiler
- F1 style mirrors
- Skid nation Chassis Rails
- JDM rear number plate panel
- Satin black Sun Strip
- Various decals (Green light down either side etc)

Engine Bay
- ME221 ECU
- Blue silicone engine hoses
- Blue 8.5mm HT leads
- NGK Spark Plugs
- Fast5 alloy radiator
- Ramair filter
- TD04 Turbo
- AE Motorsport Intercooler (with custom hard piping)
- Turbo smart IWG75 Actuator
- Adjustable cam pulleys
- Cut rocker top
- Skidnation coolant neck blank
- Skidnation coolant reroute
- Oil cooler
- HKS Oil filters
- Red 80% Duraflex engine mounts
- Stage 3 paddle clutch
- Oil Catch can
- White Perspex slam panel and scuttle panel
- Malian Turbo-back exhaust
- Strut brace

Interior
- Micro RS1 Bucket Seats (black and yellow)
- Luke 4 Point Harness'
- TR Lane Half Cage
- DND Sports Steering Wheel
- D1 Spec Boss Kit
- Recycled plastic gear knob
- Fast 5 Door Bars
- Center Console Delete
- Unicorn Door Cards
- AEM AFR gauge

I would like to thank the following Companies/people for there help and services
Green light Insurance - Stefan Hobman Photography - GSM Performance - Bofi Racing
Viral Vinyl UK - FPM - ScullFab - Skidnation- And of course Ebay!

Rory Mcewing
Subaru Impreza WRX STi Type UK

Instagram: @rorymce
Photographer: @lomotive_ukmedia

Author Paul Doherty

Back in 2015, I was on the hunt for an Impreza. From young, I've always loved the blue/gold Subaru look (who doesn't?!) and ever since I've aspired to own one.

While looking this white Hawkeye came up for sale, you hardly ever see these come up for sale in the UK and I'd never really seen them around. It took my interest and I had to go see it. 200 miles later, I couldn't fault it. The seller was passionate, he cared for the car and gave it anything it needed. I couldn't walk away.

Next thing I know I own a white Subaru Impreza!
It was bought standard and that's how I planned on keeping it. The previous cars I had done some minor modifications, lowered suspension, splitters, nothing major but the difference this time was the car.

My previous cars didn't excite me like this one, as I'm sure you would agree - Yaris, Corsa, 207 ... not the most exciting cars compared to the world-famous Subaru Impreza.

The car has been through various different looks over the years as you can imagine after owning it for 5 years but the look it has now I think is the one which will stay for a while, I love it.

Here's my Subaru Impreza WRX STi Type UK, as you can see it's not your normal Subaru, it's had a few modifications.

Interior
- Bride and Takata seat setup
- ABC pillar and roof Alcantara wrapped
- All blue STi items switched for black or grey alternatives
- Rear bench removed
- Alpine speakers throughout with hidden amp

Exterior
- Airlift performance suspension
- SSR SP1 fully rebuilt polished wheels
- Full charge speed style lower lip kit
- Custom rear diffuser
- Smoothed boot
- C style headlights

My Favourite modification has to be the Air ride. This is my first car on air, the confusion when aired out from people who don't understand is always funny!

I've never had a car like this, a normal Subaru turns heads anywhere it goes because of the very distinctive exhaust note. Add to that a clean, white, low Impreza and people seem to love it!

There's not much left to do ... it's had various looks over the years but I think I'm finished. Check out my Instagram to see the various different looks over the years @rorymce

Instagram: @short_back_and_sideways.
Photographer: @angell_photography_

Nick Lynch
Modified Mk2.5 1.8vvt MX5

Author: Paul Doherty

I'm a 26 year old carpenter from Bedfordshire, I run a car club called Fuelled Collective and have been in the scene for around 15 years. I think the reason I'm into the street scene is purely the fault of Need for Speed.

That game was life as a kid growing up loving cars and stuff. Also playing on that "car town" mat we all had as kids, lining the cars up alongside the roads and racing 2 cars sliding them round the roundabout! Oh the memories, now I do it for real!

Fast and furious probably didn't help either and as long as I can remember I've always wanted a little sports car with a huge bodykit and BGW..... so I guess I've kinda achieved a childhood dream with my current build.

I was always going to be a petrol head i think. It's in my blood. I own a modified Mk4 Astra van and a highly Modified Mk2.5 1.8vvt MX5.

The van is supposed to be a workhorse but gets used for other stuff too. The mx5 is a toy, bought with the intentions of becoming a drift missile but somehow turned into a show car as well as a drift toy.

The car was originally stock at 146bhp, but has since been boosted with an Eaton m45 supercharger putting it up over 200 Bhp. Exact numbers will be known after remapping.

The car has been built on my driveway with limited tools and even less knowledge by myself and my partner! It's been an experience but we are loving doing it! The paint works done by Offbeat Customs (@uk_obc) tints by Capacita Customs (@CapacitaCustoms) and 7Eleven detailing (@7eleven_detailing) provide the goods to keep her clean.

This has been both of our first full project builds so lots of learning curves along the way but the process has been incredible! Lots of mixed emotions and long, stressful times lol but with the help and advice of some friends we have got through everything! Although the car is FAR from finished still! So far it's been just over 2 years in the making! As founder of Fuelled Collective i can't wait to get back to normal with show season etc and show off the hard work we have put into this build with the club at shows and our weekly Tuesday evening meets in Bedford. @fuelledcollective.

We are hoping to see the car competing in Formula G in the next year or so, but we are seeing how the build goes before getting into it as we may end up building a second boosted mx5 for that. Time will tell! The car will be attending most shows including but not limited to..... Japfests, Japshows, mod nats, fast shows, Trax's, jdm Combe. Basically any and all we can get to.

My dream car is a Ferrari f40 but seeing as I'd have to sell both arms and legs for that, and then wouldn't be able to drive I'd settle for a nicely tuned/modified mk4 supra!

ANGELL
Photography

Mod list includes:

- Carbon miata wide arch kit with Grams diffuser and custom splitter.
- Rear window blackout, headlight tints and eyebrows by capacita custom
- M45 supercharger with KAVS 17% pulley and Forge BOV
- Twin exit catback with japspeed decat midsection, manifold on way
- Salon motor sports mounting bracket/auto tensioner plate
- SVT big brake upgrade with stainless steel braided lines
- Hardtop roof with Jass performance hard mounts
- Red painted upper/lower arms, anti roll bars etc
- Swapped out door cards with red fabric
- Full custom respray by offbeat customs
- Suntrip and Fuelled Collective graphics over
- TRD 90mm deep dish steering wheel
- Custom painted interior trim and console
- Dave Fab screen washer bottle relocation
- Android double din touch screen head unit
- Projector COB angel eye fog lights
- Japspeed carbon fibre BGW
- FK bucket seats with harnesses
- Charcoal chamber removal
- Rota Kyusha 15" 8j alloys + 15" 9j
- Chrome red door catch covers
- Rocker switch/start button
- 20mm and 30mm spacers
- Wheel nuts and dust caps
- Uprated silicone hose kit
- Red screen wash jet hoses
- Interior foot well LED
- Lowered on coilovers
- After market gear knob
- TR Lane harness bar
- Custom dmax bonnet
- Rear bumper cut
- Uprated speakers
- NRG short boss
- Under car lighting
- ITG cone filter
- LED twin USB slot
- ABS removal
- ME221 ECU
- RX8 yellow injectors
- Grams roof spoiler
- FMIC

And more with MUCH MUCH more to come still!!
Including twin rear calipers set up, hydro handbrake, full roll cage, new bucket seats and harnesses and graphics kit!

ANGELL *Photography*

Bob Morgan
Nissan Skyline R33 GTST

Author: Carla De Freitas

I'm aged 33, I live in sunny Devon, near Exeter after moving from Wales to live with my fiancée. I currently work as an assistant manager in a pub/hotel what got me into the car scene? My dad got me into the car scene and my love for cars, I would watch formula one and touring cars on TV with him and go to car shows with him and his classic mini.

My first car was a classic mini 1986, which I modified then I got a proton Satria which I absolutely loved, unfortunately, a motorway accident caused the car to be written off, so I decided to buy another Proton, which was featured in lots of magazines after I did a lot of modifications to it such as supercharger, nitrous etc.

My current pride and joy that has caused many headaches is a Nissan Skyline R33 GTST which I purchased for £2,069 back in 2011. It had a couple of mods when I bought it, it had a standard turbo stage 1 tuned. In those 9 years since I have had the car, I have modified it quite a lot.

I am the owner of Midnight44club, we can be found on Facebook, search midnight 44 club and Instagram @midnight44club. The link for our YouTube page is Midnight 44 Club, we attend many shows and have won several trophies as a club and on my own. My dream car has always been a Skyline after playing Gran Turismo on the original PlayStation as a kid.

Most of the work I have done myself, but the tuning has been done by 'Whifbitz' in Caldicot. Parts for the build have come from 'Auto-Extreme', 'JDM garage' and 'Conceptua tuning'.

I have been through several stages of tune, and I managed a 13second 1/4mile 115mph @ 480 BHP at Santa Pod raceway.

Currently the cars last dyno reading was 579 BHP which is 483.2 BHP 368.6LB-FT @ the hubs @ 1.2bar. I started making changes to the engine/drive train after being beaten on the drag strip by a 70 year old lady driving a Rover 75 on the drag strip at Santa Pod, the video can be found on YouTube, I am still friends with her and her family and still joke about me now.

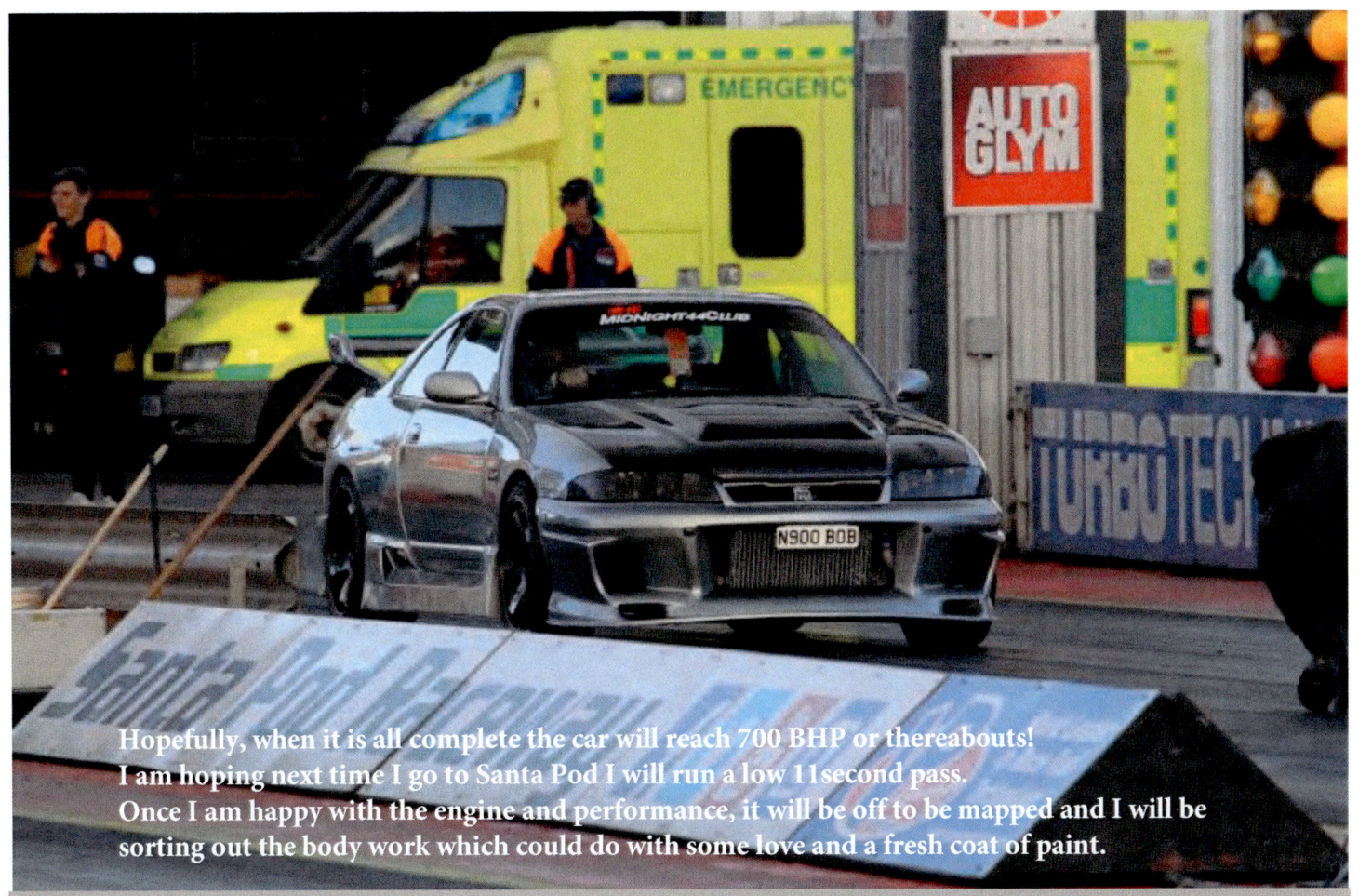

Hopefully, when it is all complete the car will reach 700 BHP or thereabouts! I am hoping next time I go to Santa Pod I will run a low 11second pass. Once I am happy with the engine and performance, it will be off to be mapped and I will be sorting out the body work which could do with some love and a fresh coat of paint.

Engine:
Petrol blue cam cover bolts & blue dress-up washers
Kandy blue rocker covers with lightning graphics
Carbon fibre cooling panel
An-10 GReddy oil cooler kit
Freddy intake plenum
Turbo smart 1200 fpr
Torques fuel filter with 10-micron element
Hel an-8 Teflon braided feed fuel line
Hel An-6 Teflon braided fuel return line
HKS earthing / grounding kit
Japspeed alloy radiator
Carbon fibre strut brace
90mm throttle body
Boost junkie's silicone hoses
Brake stopper
3-inch inlet/outlet Aluminium intercooler with custom made pipework
K&N air filter
Bosh 1000cc top feed fuel injectors
Billet fuel rail
Holset hx35/40 modified turbocharger with bigger billet comp wheel
Custom Aluminium power steering reservoir
Custom screen wash reservoir
Aluminium An-10 oil catch tank
An-10 stainless breather pipes
Rb26dett long nose crankshaft
Rb26dett Manley con rods
Rb26dett Manley con rods
Rb26dett long nose crankshaft
Rb26dett Manley con rods
Rb26dett oversized Cp pistons 87mm
Rb25det head with 1.6mm Cosworth head gasket
Uprated intake and exhaust Supertech valve stem seals
Acl race bearings (big end and mains)
R35 GTR Coil pack conversion kit
Hel braided turbo oil lines
N1 oil pump
N1 water pump
Engine fully balanced
Tomei poncams
Tomei oil restrictor
Link g4+ ECU system
AEM cas trigger disk
Engine torque damper
Twin Turbosmart 40mm waste gates
Hybrid performance steam pipe exhaust manifold
HKS dump valve
Walbro F90000274 (455LPH) Fuel Pump with Direct Feed Separate Relay Wiring
Custom 3-inch turbo-back exhaust system 5-inch exit
Screamer pipes by side skirt
Orc 559 twin-plate clutch
MRL Stainless Steel Braided Clutch Line Reservoir to Slave Cylinder
Supra exhaust manifold studs

Brakes, suspension, Wheels:
- BC Racing Adjustable Suspension: Set Soft On the Rear & Medium On The Front
- Driftworks Hicas eliminator kit
- Hel blue braided brake lines
- Front and rear strut braces
- Ferodo DS2000 Front & Rear Brake Pads
- Brembo rear grooved brake disks
- The electronic Line lock system
- 30mm hub centric wheel spacers on the rear
- Big front brake disk conversion
- 18" X 9.5 ET30 Gunmetal Rota GTR Alloy Wheels

Interior / Exterior

R32 GTR front seats
GTR Middlehurst floor mats
Sunroof solar panel and headlining replaced with a non-sunroof model
R33 GTR clock clusters
Nismo Carbon Gear knob
Bride gear knob and handbrake covers
Auto Meter Monster Rev Counter with shift light
Auto Meter Turbo Timer
Snap off steering wheel
Sony rear speakers with kicker front speakers
Cusco dash dodger roll cage
Tablet to use as ECU display and run iTunes
Do Luck front and rear bumpers
Blue air horn
Tinted modified headlights with devil eyes
Hornet Maxx 1 alarm system.
Tablet to use as ECU display and run iTunes
Do Luck front and rear bumpers
Blue air horn
Tinted modified headlights with devil eyes
Rover mini side indicators on the front bumper
Greddy gracer side skirts
Nismo tinted side indicators
Vented front wings 25mm wider
Ganador Rare E-01261 mirrors
APR Carbon fibre Big Gay Wing
Nismo carbon fibre bonnet with aero catches
Fibreglass flush fit the boot lid
light up rear skyline panel
fog light removed and installed in offside rear tail light
R33 GTR carbon fibre grille
R33 GTR rear over fenders
R33 GTR fuel flap
Hornet Maxx 1 alarm system.

Thomas Vo
1976 Datsun 280z

Instagram: @aivothom and @ryujin_Z.
Photographer: @fireblazinmedia

Author: Pablo Colon

I'm currently a student at University of Buffalo for Computer Science and Mathematics, and I own a Vietnamese restaurant and a photography business which I do on the side whenever I have free time. My photography mainly consists of portraits, street/urban and automotive.

I became interested in cars at a young age due to my fathers influence. He was an automotive enthusiast before I was born, owning mainly American muscle and some 90's JDM cars. Growing up as a kid, I was rewarded with hot wheels for doing well in school, or finishing chores so I was very interested in cars, I was that child who grew up working on cars with my father, from holding the flashlight to actually working on the cars with him.

It was a good bonding experience. The car scene currently isn't the same as it was in the past 10 years, nowadays I don't see as much passion for cars as I do the need for attention and "clout" on social media.

The Datsun S30 chassis has been my favourite car growing up, from seeing photos in magazines such as Import Tuner, to mangas such as Wangan Midnight. After a successful year in the restaurant business and my photography picking up, I was finally able to afford a project car and decided it was time to check one dream car off my list.

I chose the 280z instead of the 240z because the availability of the 280z was greater than the 240z, and honestly I couldn't afford a clean rust free 240z.

I'm not a purist of any sort but I would not want to "ruin" a clean 240z. In my honest opinion, the 280z is the car to "Resto-Mod". Some other cars I would eventually like to own would be an R32 GTR, a real Fairlady 240z, and a Porsche 911.

So I bought the car sight unseen as it was during the 2020 Covid Quarantine in the USA, the car was originally from Tampa, FL and I live in Buffalo, NY. I paid a Datsun specialist in the area to do a PPI (Pre-Purchase Inspection) on the car as I could not check it out in person and the car checked out, it was healthy, well maintained and had little to no rust in the common areas. The Datsun S30's are amazing cars to drive, and those who have driven one will understand what I mean.

The car provides a raw driving experience with no electronic assistance, and you feel as if you are in full control of the car with no assistance such as abs, traction control, power steering, etc.

Owning a car like this is an experience in itself, from being stopped at gas stations by people to talk about how they had one 30-40 years ago or how their parents or grandparents had one, or asking me what kind of car this is and how they're shocked to find out it is a Datsun from the 70's. Most people nowadays don't even know or remember Datsun.

My plans for the car are to build a fun street car that I can enjoy and drive to the track, I do not plan on building a crazy high horsepower car, or a fully dedicated track car. I want to be able to enjoy the car on the street as much as I would on a track. In the future I am planning on rebuilding the motor to handle a little bit more power reliably, and my goals are to hit at least 450whp.

I also plan on getting the full suspension/chassis components from Apex Engineered to modernize the suspension. Ohm from Apex Engineered is an amazing guy, and all the products AE provides are the best money can buy and his customer service is top notch. If you're thinking about replacing any suspension parts for your Datsun and many other cars you will not regret going with Apex Engineered.

Suspension:
- After market Springs and Shocks,
- Planning on switching over to a true coilovers set up.
- (BC coilovers),
- Garage Theory Strut Bar

Wheels:
- Rota Grids 16x8 +0,
- Toyo Proxy R1R 225/45/16

Interior:
- NRG 350mm Deep Dish Steering Wheel with short hub and quick release,
- AGI Roll Bar/cage,
- Autometer Gauges,
- Night runner x Willians Harnesses

Exterior:
- Carbon Fiber Front and Rear Bumpers,
- Carbon Fiber Spoiler,
- Dapper Lighting LED SEVEN Headlights

Engine/Drive train:
- RB25DET Series 2,
- R33 5-speed,
- 3.9 R200 LSD,
- RSEnthalpy Tune (295whp 285 ft/lb),
- Greddy Intake Manifold,
- GTR Coil Packs,
- ARP Head studs,
- ACT Stage 2 Clutch,
- Tial BOV,
- CUBE Short Shifter,

Future Plans:
Recaro Pole Positions, Garrett GTX3076r or G30 660 plus supporting mods,, Haltech ECU, Carbon Signal Moonbeam Body Kit, BC Coils. Work Meister CR01 or TE37V.

Full Vinyl wrap in Inozetek Metallic Midnight Purple. Full Front and Rear Apex Engineered Suspension/Chassis, Hoping to rebuild the motor with forged internals to handle over 500hp. Goal is to hit at least 450whp with the built motor.

STANCEAUTOMAG | PABLO COLON

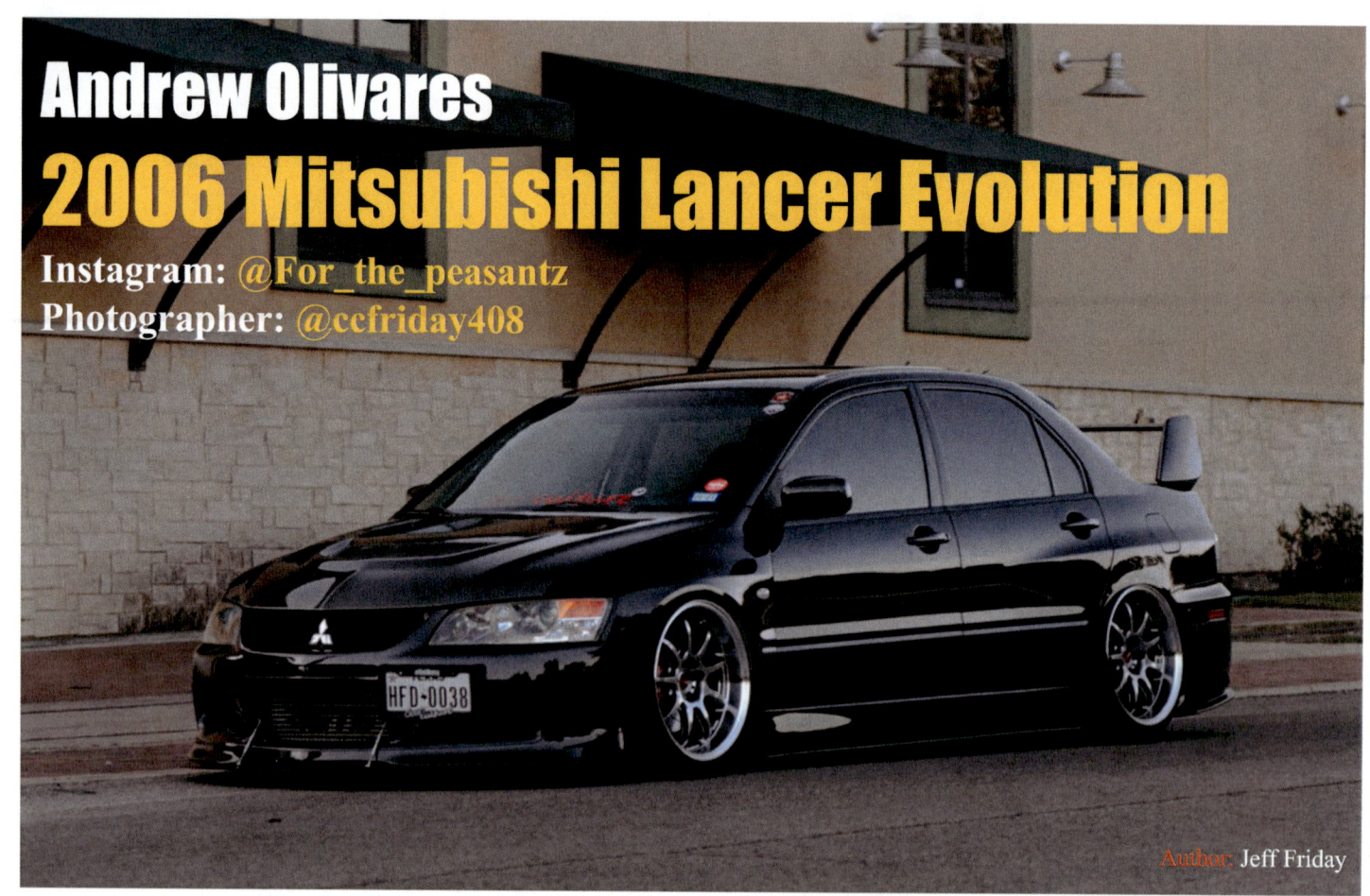

Andrew Olivares
2006 Mitsubishi Lancer Evolution

Instagram: @For_the_peasantz
Photographer: @ccfriday408

Author: Jeff Friday

My earliest memories as a child have all been car-related from going to the Drag races, getting picked up every day at school in a 1967 Ford Mustang to working underneath my dad's 1970 Oldsmobile cutlass.

At this point in my childhood, we had owned a 1967 Ford Mustang, 1968 Ford Mustang, 1992 5.0 convertible Mustang, and a 1970 Oldsmobile cutlass. So you can say I was born with motor oil running through my veins!

My biggest inspirer's were my parents, they would continue to motivate me to do better and to chase my passion with working and modifying cars so I did and the outcome has been more than rewarding! I turned my passion for working on cars into a career right after high school when I started working for an auto body shop as a painter's helper and excelled on becoming a body technician. I have fixed and worked on many cars but there was one car I had the opportunity of repairing that blew me out of the water!

The pure rawness yet exhilarating feeling of a Mitsubishi Lancer Evolution 8 at this point I was hooked and it became my dream car. A year after experiencing and driving an Evolution I had Moved to Anchorage, Alaska and started working at a Subaru Dealership, my wife and I were expecting our first child and in desperate need of a four-door family car after looking for another 6 months we had come across A 2006 Mitsubishi Lancer Evolution IX SE (My dream car) with 4,000 miles on it, after inquiring about the vehicle it turned out a 75-year-old man had owned it and was on consignment at a lot! Nothing had been done to it fully stock still had the new car smell, at the time of purchase I really couldn't afford the car financially but my wife looked at me and said we will make it happen don't worry!

After making my last payment on my Evolution IX SE I had started to modify it to my liking! I had built this car all in my garage, I fully built the motor with a long rod set up using Wiseco pistons, Manley I-beam rods, ACL race bearings, ported cylinder head titanium valve springs with retainers, 274 GSC cam's, ported stock intake manifold and exhaust manifold, GT3582r Precision turbo, ETS front mount with ETS short route charge pipes, Tial bov, HKS Turbo-back exhaust. The transmission is a fully built jacks trans with Exedy triple disk clutch.

The Suspension is a full Airlift 3H System with dual compressors and a 5 gallon brushed aluminium tank, full GT Spec under bracing, fender bracing, and trunk bracing. Exterior consist of Work D9R wheels with Hankook Ventus v12 evo2 tires, APR carbon fibre front splitter, Rexpeed carbon fibre side skirt extensions, Rexpeed carbon fibre rear bumper extensions, Seibon carbon fibre hood, HIC rear window deflector, and STOCK OEM tarmac black paint the car has never been repainted.

The interior of the Evo is the next on the list to concentrate on currently I have the stock OEM Recaro seats with Nardi detachable deep corn suede steering wheel 330mm, Prosport fully digital gauges with AEM uego wide band, Double din entertainment system with JL audio speakers. The headliner A, B, and C pillars will soon be all Alcantara with red accent stitching.

My future plans for this car are endless the only thing I will not do is ruin the perfect body of a Mitsubishi Evolution IX (wide body). Always remember why stop when you can do better and don't only motivate yourself and motivate others around you! My goal for the car has always been the same SIMPLY CLEAN!

STANCEAUTOMAG|JEFF FRIDAY

Exterior
- APR carbon front splitter
- Seibon carbon fibre hood
- Rexpeed carbon fibre side skirt extenders
- Rexpeed carbon fibre rear bumper extenders
- HIC rear window deflector

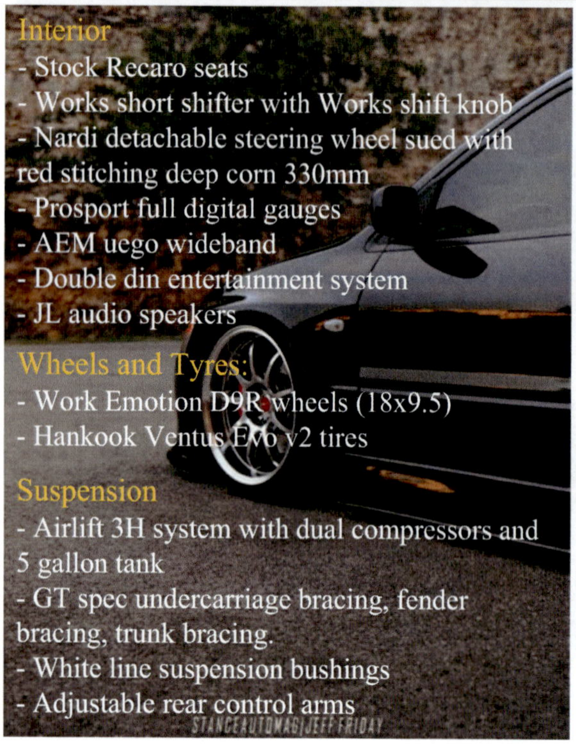

Interior
- Stock Recaro seats
- Works short shifter with Works shift knob
- Nardi detachable steering wheel sued with red stitching deep corn 330mm
- Prosport full digital gauges
- AEM uego wideband
- Double din entertainment system
- JL audio speakers

Wheels and Tyres:
- Work Emotion D9R wheels (18x9.5)
- Hankook Ventus Evo v2 tires

Suspension
- Airlift 3H system with dual compressors and 5 gallon tank
- GT spec undercarriage bracing, fender bracing, trunk bracing.
- White line suspension bushings
- Adjustable rear control arms

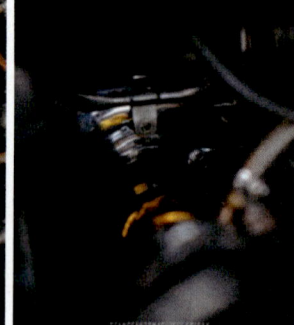

Engine/Transmission
- Fully built 2.0 long rod short block
- Wiseco HD2 pistons
- Manley I-beam rods
- ACL race bearings
- Manley turbo tuff crank
- Ported cylinder head
- GSC +1MM valves, Titanium springs and retainers
- GSC 274 camshafts
- ARP head studs
- GT3582R precision Turbo
- Ported Intake and Exhaust manifold
- ETS front mount with short route piping
- Mishimoto radiator
- Tial 50mm bov
- Map performance turbo down pipe 1pc waste gate dumped
- HKS HI-Power exhaust system
- ARC exhaust manifold heat shield
- Jacks built transmission
- Jacks built center diff